POLICY AND PRACTIC.
NUMBER FOURTEEN

Individual Outcomes:
Getting Back to What Matters

POLICY AND PRACTICE IN HEALTH AND SOCIAL CARE

POLICY AND PRACTICE IN HEALTH AND SOCIAL CARE
SERIES EDITORS
JOYCE CAVAYE and ALISON PETCH

Individual Outcomes: Getting Back to What Matters

Dr Emma Miller
Honorary Senior Research Fellow,
Glasgow School of Social Work,
University of Strathclyde

DUNEDIN

Published by
Dunedin Academic Press Ltd
Hudson House
8 Albany Street
Edinburgh EH1 3QB
Scotland

First published 2012

ISBN: 978–1–906716–30–1
ISSN: 1750–1407

British Library Cataloguing in Publication data
A catalogue record for this book is available at the British Library

Typeset by Makar Publishing Production, Edinburgh
Printed in Great Britain by CPI Antony Rowe

CONTENTS

It gives particular pleasure to introduce this volume on personal outcomes. It is the result of the author's involvement with this issue over a lengthy period during which she has been at the forefront of exploring the detail of this approach, initially as a researcher and subsequently working closely alongside partnerships in Scotland to embed the approach in routine practice. The evolution of personal outcomes provides a fascinating case study of knowledge translation, building from an evidence base of extensive research to the current adoption of elements of a personal-outcomes approach across the vast majority of partnerships in Scotland. It highlights both the need for and the benefits of an extended timescale in the evolution of policy into practice.

A vocabulary of outcomes and of the need for an outcomes-based approach has featured strongly at both central and local levels in recent years. Beyond the words, however, there has often been uncertainty as to exactly what such an approach might look like and how it can be achieved. The author's experience of working closely with practitioners across a large number of agencies, as they wrestle with these issues, has given her both a unique insight into the challenges that need to be met and an invaluable pool of strategies and resources that have evolved in response to them.

A particular feature of this volume is its holistic approach to the exploration of outcomes, placing the discussion of the intricacies of the specific methodology within a broader discussion of the role of the welfare state and of current policy tensions between management and relationship-led approaches. It also addresses the importance of considering personal outcomes from the perspective of different stakeholders: those who access support; unpaid carers; and staff involved in the provision of support. The essential contribution of leadership from middle management and of ownership from senior management is highlighted.

It is hoped that this volume will play its part in ensuring that the achievement of personal outcomes becomes the core driver at the heart of health and social care policy and practice.

Dr Joyce Cavaye
Faculty of Health and Social Care,
The Open University in Scotland,
Edinburgh

Professor Alison Petch
The Institute for Research and
Innovation in Social Services (IRISS),
Glasgow

ACKNOWLEDGEMENTS

I would like to acknowledge Ailsa Cook who has worked with me since 2004, and colleagues at the Glasgow School of Social Work for the support and laughter enjoyed at writers retreats during 2010–11.

The content of this book has been shaped and influenced by a very large number of people from a range of agencies across Scotland. These contributors are too numerous to be named individually, and include people who use services, carers and staff, and many people who have come into two or all three of these categories during the past few years. The commitment of so many people to improve things for the greater good, in the face of adversity, is a continuing inspiration.

GLOSSARY OF ABBREVIATIONS

ADHD	Attention Deficit Hyperactivity Disorder
ARCG	Assessment Review Co-ordinating Group
CCBN	Community Care Benchmarking Network
CCOF	Community Care Outcomes Framework
CCPS	Community Care Providers Scotland (latterly Coalition of Care and Support Providers in Scotland)
CDSET	Carer Defined Service Evaluation Toolkit
CHCP	Community Health and Care Partnership
CHP	Community Health Partnership
CIPFA	Chartered Institute of Public Finance and Accountancy
COSLA	Convention of Scottish Local Authorities
CSCI	Commission for Social Care Inspection
DH	Department of Health (England and Wales)
DHSS	Department of Health and Social Security
FACS	Fair Access to Care Services
GP	General Practitioner
HEAT	Health Efficiency Access Treatment
IRISS	Institute for Research and Innovation in Social Services
JIT	Joint Improvement Team of the Scottish Government
JPIAF	Joint Performance Information and Assessment Framework
MASC	Modernising Adult Social Care
ME	Myalgic Encephalomyelitis
NCOs	National Carers Organisations
NHS	National Health Service
NMIS	National Minimum Information Standards
NOF	National Outcomes Framework
PA	Personal Assistant
PROMs	Patient Reported Outcome Measures
PSSRU	Personal Social Service Research Unit

RCN   Royal College of Nursing
SG   Scottish Government
SOA   Single Outcome Agreement
SPRU   Social Policy Research Unit
SDO   Service Delivery and Organisation
SSA   Single Shared Assessment
SSI   Social Services Inspectorate
UDSET   User Defined Service Evaluation Toolkit
VOCAL   Voice of Carers Across Lothian

INTRODUCTION

Personal outcomes, or what matters to people who use services and their carers, are relatively straightforward concepts. Research consistently confirms the importance of outcomes such as feeling safe and secure, being able to get out and about and being listened to. However, maintaining a focus on these outcomes in practice proves more challenging than might be assumed. This book is largely based on experience of developing and implementing a knowledge-exchange programme in health and social care in Scotland. The work started in 2004, with a two-year Department of Health (DH) funded research project on outcomes for people who use services delivered in partnership by health and social care. The findings from this research were subsequently to form the foundations for the knowledge-exchange programme, which started on a small scale in 2006 and has continued to develop and expand since. Sponsored by the Joint Improvement Team (JIT) of the Scottish Government, the programme has developed in partnership between the researchers, local health and social care partnerships, provider agencies and service users and carers. In order to appreciate how outcomes, or what matters to people, can be placed at the centre of systems, it is necessary to understand how these outcomes translate into practice from each perspective. Where barriers are identified, the role of champions from each group comes into its own, in the search for creative solutions. As local organisations continue to grapple with the outcomes agenda, this book pulls together some of the learning from the programme to date, highlighting barriers, solutions and benefits as well as cautionary notes with regard to different interpretations of outcomes.

Understanding why it is such a challenge to maintain a focus on what matters to people in health and social care system requires an exploration of the context in which services operate. Chapter 1 reviews the development of the welfare state in the UK, acknowledging some inherent contradictions, with emphasis on community care policy over the past twenty years. There is a particular focus on assessment, including divergent policy between the devolved administrations in the UK. The chapter will highlight policy tensions around partnership working and outcomes, including some of the associated contradictions experienced by staff at the front line, and the impact on user and carer involvement in decision-making. The chapter introduces the knowledge-exchange programme on outcomes, setting the scene for the subsequent chapters.

Chapter 2 begins with a review of the Department of Health research on outcomes, and previous research at the University of York. This will highlight the solid evidence base about what matters to people using health and social care services, including some differences between groups of users. The chapter will link into the current work with the Joint Improvement Team, introducing some of the early barriers to implementation, and evidence of how the focus on outcomes is enabling user perspectives to shape service provision. The chapter will also introduce two paradigms that influence health and social care, which can result in outcomes being interpreted in different ways. This includes reference to differing interpretations of the concept of personalisation.

Chapter 3 on carers highlights significant and long-standing issues regarding the role and perspectives of unpaid carers, in relation to the outcomes agenda. Gate-keeping concerns of staff tend to crystallise in attitudes towards carers, with widespread reluctance to engage for fear of 'raising expectations' and having insufficient services to offer. However, addressing carers' outcomes is essential to avoid further demands on services further down the line.

Understanding staff perspectives is critical if outcomes-based working is to be successfully implemented. Better outcomes for staff are also a prerequisite if the outcomes agenda is to succeed. Chapter 4 will include brief consideration of concepts of power and the notion of the street-level bureaucrat. Developing themes raised in the first chapter, Chapter 4 will identify how staff are caught between a variety of competing imperatives which sometimes conflict with their values. One of the key message from staff has been that organisational buy-in to the outcomes agenda is essential.

Chapter 5 identifies the critical role of leadership by middle management, as well as visible and active ownership at senior management level. Organisations are constantly juggling a variety of competing imperatives and demands. With brief reference to different approaches being adopted in Scotland, the chapter will highlight the need to keep the person at the centre amidst these competing and sometimes conflicting demands.

Chapter 6 includes a review of current policy in Scotland relevant to the outcomes theme. The book will conclude by reflecting back on key considerations, including the continuing need to join up policy at the centre. Particular emphasis is placed on the need to ensure that managerialist tendencies are prevented from eclipsing relationship-based approaches, which focus on the outcomes important to people.

CHAPTER 1

Exploring the Policy Context to Health and Social Care Assessment and Practice

> Outcomes are defined as the impact, effect or consequence of a service or policy. Outcomes focused services are therefore those that meet the goals, aspirations or priorities of individual service users. They can be contrasted with services whose goals, content or mode of delivery are standardised, regardless of the circumstances of those who use them; or are determined primarily by commissioners or providers rather than users. Outcomes focused services are therefore by implication also personalised. (Glendinning *et al.*, 2008, p. 55)

The concept of outcomes has become increasingly prevalent in policy and practice terms in the early twenty-first century. The generalised policy goal of improving outcomes for people who use services is not new, and has for some time been accompanied by a sense that an outcomes focus will support achievement of elusive goals such as user involvement, partnership working and user satisfaction. More recently, against a context of concerns about demographic pressures, the potential of outcomes-based working to maximise independence and build on the assets of people using services has resulted in the concept itself moving centre stage. At the same time, the concept of outcomes is associated with managerialist concerns for accountability and performance management in the public sector. This opening chapter will set the context for an exploration of outcomes-based working, particularly in relation to health and social care. This will set the scene for consideration of the perspectives of the range of stakeholders in the system, with the aim of trying to support a common understanding of the potential and pitfalls of the outcomes agenda. This will include discussion of the tensions between managerialist and relationship-based perspectives on outcomes. First, this chapter will consider the context of health and social care services in the UK in the postwar era. Understanding the context of how services are organised and some of the competing priorities involved is necessary to investigate different interpretations of outcomes.

Post-1945 development of the welfare state

The health care system of any country has a significant role in defining its character, particularly given the direct link to life itself, sending out important signals about societal values. In the UK, the National Health Service (NHS) came into being on 5 July 1948, the first health system in any Western society to offer free health care to an entire population. One of the reasons why the NHS is so highly valued by the British public is that it resulted in a transformation of 'inadequate, partial and muddled patchworks of health care provision into a neat administrative structure' (Klein, 1995, p. 1). Established under the 1946 Act, the NHS was democratic in so far as it rested on a social and political consensus, based on the principle that the whole population should have access to health services on the basis of need, free at the point of delivery.

Although the NHS was supported by cross-party consensus, however, its existence was preceded by years of debate. There was debate within the medical profession over whether it should be controlled primarily by local or national government, which resulted in separate identities being granted to General Practitioners (GPs) as independent contractors, to hospitals and to local authority public health departments which included community nursing. At central level, the health minister was accountable to Parliament for policy and planning, and ministers could be questioned in Parliament on policy and the running of the service. Democratic accountability at the local level was, however, much weaker (Allsop, 1995).

It was some time after the NHS emerged before universal provision of social services followed. Nearly two decades later, the 1964 Kilbrandon Committee in Scotland and the 1965 Seebohm Committee in England resulted in comprehensive local authority social services. The late sixties are described as 'the high water mark of public sector social work', creating generic agencies, intended to be a fifth social service, almost on a par with health, education, social services and housing (Jordan, 2007, p. 42). Before discussing the implications of the different origins and structures of the health and social services, further consideration will be given to the context of the development of the welfare state in the late twentieth century.

While the postwar development of the welfare state in the UK is viewed as an essential step in the social progress of this country, a number of key tensions were evident from the early stages, and continue to present barriers to achieving policy aspirations to the present. As Klein (1995) argues, the debate which preceded the formation of the NHS not only represented the defence of particular interests but also different world views, which could be characterised broadly as the values of localism including responsiveness, differentiation and self-government compared to national equity, efficiency and uniformity. Additionally, despite its equitable aspirations, the welfare state was created around key assumptions about the nature of British society, the needs of its citizens and how these should be met, creating different positions in relation to welfare benefits and services

> This structure naturalised a set of social arrangements based on gender (the sexual divisions of welfare); age and able-bodiedness (the structuring of dependency) and 'race' (the identity of citizenship) and fixed them as the principles of state welfare. (Clarke and Newman, 1997, p. 2)

In addition to the social settlement which underpinned the new welfare state, Clarke and Newman (1997) highlight that the organisational settlement was constructed around two modes of co-ordination — bureaucratic administration and professionalism. While bureaucracy offered the appeal of predictability, stability and neutrality, professionalism was based on standardisation of skills through externally controlled training and qualification (Mintzberg,

1983). These themes will be explored further in subsequent chapters, with particular interest in where the various influences converge in paternalistic tendencies in the public sector.

For many years after the NHS came into being, there was consensus about its role and place. Following the ideas of economist Maynard Keynes (1936), cross-party political support for public services continued until the financial crisis of the early 1970s. At this stage, the monetarist ideas of Milton Friedman, from the University of Chicago, took hold. Friedman argued against investing in the public sector to create employment, supporting an alternative *laissez-faire* approach treating the public sector as a free market that should be allowed to run its self-correcting course (Seddon, 2008). Margaret Thatcher brought monetarist ideas into the political mainstream from 1979, liberalising the nationalised industries and introducing the 'quasi-market' into public services. Central to the monetarist approach was public choice theory, based on a belief that human beings are fundamentally self-interested, and that incentives need to be aligned to motivate self-interest. To make quasi-markets work, performance has to be evaluated and incentivised to exploit selfishly competitive behaviour (Seddon, 2008). Such macro-economic theories matter because their influence pervades services, playing out in interactions between staff and the public, as will be discussed in the next three chapters.

The health and social care divide

Within the welfare state, the way that the NHS and social services developed as separate entities has served to increase the complexity of service delivery, and how services are experienced by the public, particularly in the realm of health and social care. There is limited space available here to review the history of this divide, with accounts available elsewhere (Means *et al.*, 2008; Petch, 2008). With regard to structural divisions, separate identities within the NHS have already been noted, as has the subsequent and largely distinct development of social services.

Financial arrangements surrounding health and social care play a significant role in maintaining tensions between the sectors, particularly because the resources available to deliver services to the public have always been subject to limitations. An enduring tension between health and social care is that care needs defined as 'health care' are provided free of charge, while those defined as 'social care' are subject to means testing and charges to the individual. Although, as highlighted by Means *et al.* (2008), there has been periodic interest in health and social care provision for the groups of the population traditionally served by health and social care, or the less politically salient needs (Bruce and Forbes, 2005) of 'Cinderella' groups, the overall history is one of neglect. This is not just an issue between health and social care, but also within the NHS where there is a tendency for secondary care to retain resources. Such tensions manifest in various forms, perhaps most sharply at the interface between acute and community sectors, including in relation to delayed discharge from hospital beds, due to difficulties in identifying suitable alternatives (Petch, 2008).

Given the considerable complexity of bridging the divide between health and social care, it is perhaps unsurprising that housing has tended to remain a relatively neglected partner. Despite attempts by government in the 1990s to progress integration of housing with health and social care, caution has more recently been expressed about the prospects of this agenda (Means *et al.*, 2008). In Scotland, although housing has tended to be the forgotten relation in the partnership agenda (Petch, 2008), there are now joint social work and health departments in several areas. A recent policy agenda that has emerged in Scotland in response to demographic concerns is Reshaping Care for Older People, which includes a workstream on supported housing (Scottish Government, 2011). Given the continuing financial crisis, it will become increasingly necessary for health, social care, housing and other sectors to work collaboratively.

Further tensions between health and care centre around cultural issues, with differential emphases on the medical and social models of care. Again, tensions are not delineated simply by health versus social care sectors, but vary according to which sector of the health or indeed social service is under consideration. The medical model views illness or impairment as the result of personal tragedy and is mainly associated with institutional care, whereas the social model locates the barriers which disabled people face in societal structures and processes which privilege people who are able bodied and healthy. The social model has aimed to shift attitudes towards a position whereby people with disabilities should be supported to lead an active and full life, and should have a voice in shaping the support they receive. There has been progress with challenging paternalistic attitudes within services (Tudor Hart, 2006), supported by a shift of function within the NHS, which was originally set up to manage disease and acute illness, but has increasingly moved towards managing long-term conditions, and a commensurate need for community-based services. In this context, the need for a different relationship between staff and users and carers is evident (Burns, 2009).

Despite the range of constraints to effective joint working between health and social care, partnership working was given renewed emphasis by the New Labour government, which came into power in 1997. A more recent review of the evidence confirmed that 'closer and more effective working between health and social care will best be progressed by a focus on partnership working at the team and organisational level rather than structural change at the macro level' (Petch 2011, p. 7). Partnership working remains a theme across the UK at the time of writing. Having briefly considered the early years of the welfare state in the UK, attention will now shift to the 1990 Act.

1990 NHS and Community Care Act

The 1990 NHS and Community Care Act was the first enactment of community care as a policy in the UK, bringing in the most sweeping legislative reforms in the field since the 1940s (Kendall, 1999), including change in the way that welfare services were financed, organised and delivered (Cavaye, 2006). This watershed is viewed as a defining moment throughout this book, because of the repercussions for each set of actors involved in the system. Positive elements were contained in the greater emphasis on providing care for people in the community rather than in institutional settings.

However, the Act also reinforced existing and introduced new tensions, through redefining the boundaries between health and social care and introducing the 'quasi-market'. Through moving responsibility for community care from the NHS to social services, a boundary was created between people with specialist medical or nursing needs who were the responsibility of the NHS, which is free at the point of delivery, and those in need of community or social care for whom responsibility lies with social services departments whose services are means tested. Given that both services operate within budget restriction, this has caused long-standing tensions around whether an individual's needs are categorised as medical or social, which is not conducive to sustaining a focus on what matters to the individual using the services.

Although monetarist ideas had already entered UK public services in the 1980s, the 1990 Health and Social Care Act represents a landmark in marketisation. The New Right in Britain played a particular role in shaping neoliberal discourse, which paved the way for the changing relationship between state and market, centred around public choice theory (Niskanen, 1971). From this perspective, the monopoly position of state providers is presented as denying users of their services the opportunity to exercise customer choice. State monopolies are contrasted with the dynamic and enterprising qualities of markets in which competition guarantees choice (Clarke and Newman, 1997). Public choice provided a rationale for introducing a requirement to separate provider and purchaser functions, resulting in a well-established mixed economy in social care, and to a lesser extent in the NHS. The consequent fragmentation of service provision has resulted in continuing challenges in planning, due to insufficient information about need and supply (Wistow *et al.*, 1996), and limited responsiveness due to failure to take the knowledge of care managers into consideration (Ware *et al.*, 2003), or indeed, to consider the outcomes important to people who use the services and their carers (Petch, 2008). Further consideration will now be given to assessment and care management as defined by the 1990 Act, representing the interface between staff and service users.

Assessment and care management

The role of assessment in health and social care in the community has been an area of concern for many years. Assessment is a core component of health and social care services, representing a critical point of interaction between the professional, the person and their family. Depending on the approach adopted, this provides an opportunity for meaningful engagement with a view to identifying the priorities of the individual as well as the means of achieving those priorities. If conducted by a skilled assessor, this meaningful exchange might in itself have therapeutic benefits, as the person is encouraged to explore issues in their life and think about how they can build on their own strengths and capacities, working in partnership with services (Miller, 2010).

Before the current system of health and social care was established by the NHS and Community Care Act (DH, 1990), assessment procedures were far from perfect. There was a tendency towards service-led assessment, whereby the assessment could be shaped around matching the individual to a limited range of traditional services. The White Paper *Caring for People* (DH, 1989), which preceded the 1990 Act, emphasised that the primary objective was 'to make proper assessment of need and good case management the cornerstone of high quality care' (DH, 1989, p. 5). Following the White Paper, the 1990 Act introduced the requirement for a community care assessment, focused on identifying the needs of the individual and determining the appropriate response. Needs-led assessment was heralded as the means by which users of services would receive personalised, tailored care co-ordinated by a care manager acting as a broker on their behalf. Importantly, however, what constituted need was to be determined by the professional.

While assessment was to be used to identify needs, the concept of care management was introduced, 'to be used at the operational level to ensure service users were offered flexible packages of care which were to draw heavily on the independent sector' (Means *et al.*, 2008, p. 1). This was reportedly intended to achieve a more person-centred system of care and support. However, initially social workers, and subsequently some nursing staff, underwent a transformation in their role, whereby responsibilities were primarily administrative, centred on assessing needs and designing and monitoring care packages. Local authorities also focused far more on structures and processes than they did on outcomes, with implications for staff, users and carers (Challis, 1993; Lewis and Glennerster, 1996; Means *et al.*, 2008).

Despite the promises of the 1990 Act of a more person-centred system, lack of resources for social care in particular has increased the emphasis on rationing and targeting. Care managers have struggled with their conflicting roles as advocates for users and carers, whilst also acting as gatekeepers, restricting their ability to support the individual's choice and self-determination (Rummery, 2002). There has also been limited attention paid to monitoring and review (Bauld *et al.,* 2000), which means that the effectiveness of care packages, in terms of cost, quality and outcomes, is little understood. In the early 2000s, it was apparent throughout the UK that many of the aspirations that underpinned the 1990 Act had failed to materialise. In the next few years, the by then devolved administrations within the UK each embarked on programmes which placed renewed emphasis on partnership working through the sharing of assessment across agency boundaries in community care. These efforts will be discussed in Chapter 4. Here, consideration will be given to two predominant paradigms in health and social care, before moving on to consider the role of outcomes-based working.

Two competing paradigms
In exploring the context to health and social care in the UK, and in attempting to understand the enduring nature of the tensions highlighted thus far, two differing interpretations of partnership and policy, and latterly outcomes, emerge: the consumerist/managerialist approach and approaches centred around democratic citizenship and relationships. First, consumerism and managerialism will be considered separately as part of the same paradigm. Then the second paradigm – citizen/relationship-based approaches — is discussed.

Consumerism
Two key concepts that have been promoted alongside marketisation of public services are the characterisation of the public as demanding consumers, and the concept of choice. This chapter has already touched on the role of public-choice theory in driving marketisation, whereby, it is argued, a plurality of providers offers potential for responsiveness to the user in ways that monopoly public sector provision does not. This conceptualisation of choice is centred on contestability, whereby the individual can exit from an unsatisfactory service to choose from a range of alternatives. While public-choice theory had already begun to influence public services under

Margaret Thatcher, the redefinition of the service user as demanding consumer gathered momentum under John Major, with the introduction of the 'Patient's Charter' in 1991. Limitations of the charter were evident from the outset, however. Rather than conferring enforceable rights, it gave patients the option of complaining if a range of predetermined standards were not met. Pollitt (1994) notes that, as with many developments pushed through in the name of the consumer, the standards in the Charter only advised managers to consult consumers, with no obligation to comply with their wishes.

The limitations of consumerism have been highlighted by the user movement. Barnes and Prior (1995) argue that a simplistic notion of choice as selecting between options does not stand up to systematic analysis of the ways people interact with welfare services:

> Public services can be used in conditions which are likely to be experienced as risky, confusing and uncertain. This implies that, at the point of consumption, values such as confidence, security and trust may be more appreciated by users than the opportunity for choice ... Describing someone as a user of services is a description of a complex and shifting relationship. (Barnes and Prior, 1995, p. 58)

Very recent research, while indicating positive impacts of choice, also highlights complexities in the relationship between choice and independence, the need for good-quality information and support from advisors and the negative emotional impact of choice (Baxter *et al.*, 2011). As well as concerns about how choice is conceptualised, further tensions emerge from the fostering of a consumer culture in the NHS in particular. The NHS cannot meet all demands for healthcare, particularly as an increasing range of commercial providers enter a wider range of domains of healthcare. Corporations depend on maximising demand for their services and products and set out to generate this demand, sometimes with negative implications for public health. For example, the concept of disease mongering (Payer, 1992) emerged to describe promotion of expensive drugs by the industry for minor ailments and normal aspects of life. Unfortunate consequences of such consumerist approaches in health are expensive and unnecessary treatments, which can themselves induce ill health (Moynihan and Henry, 2006). With regard to outcomes, it is possible to conceptualise user outcomes in consumerist terms, as will be discussed in Chapter 2. Approaches based on collective voice and citizenship, on the other hand, emphasise the need to focus on shared interests to avoid exacerbating existing inequalities (Clarke and Newman, 1997).

Managerialism

The definition of managerialism, associated with the New Right and New Public Management, is understood here as:

> An overarching set of changes introduced in the UK from the 1980s onwards that involves providing effective services at lower cost through application of management techniques borrowed from business and industry. (Waine and Henderson, 2003, p. 51)

The principles of New Public Management have been characterised as boiling down to 'managers, markets and measurement' (Ferlie and Steane, 2002, p. 1461). The associated rapid growth of performance management was based on assumptions that private sector remedies and techniques could be transported into the public sector to improve efficiency and effectiveness, enhancing accountability and transparency (de Bruijn, 2002). These assumptions have been subject to much scrutiny in the literature (van Thiel and Leeuw, 2002; Barnes, 2004; McAdam *et al.*, 2005), which identifies a variety of pitfalls of performance management in the public sector including resources being diverted from service delivery, gaming the system and harmful unintended consequences.

For the purposes of this contextual chapter, the point is to indicate the links between performance management and outcomes. As the limitations of performance management continue to be highlighted, further attempts are made to develop more meaningful measures, including a view that a focus on outcomes might provide some solutions. In UK policy terms, the renewed interest in outcomes and performance management started with children's services, through Every Child Matters (HM Treasury, 2003), which set out a list of outcomes that children's services should be aiming to achieve for children. This was followed in 2005 by a social care Green Paper (DH, 2005, pp. 25–6) which proposed that in order 'to turn the vision for social care into a reality ... clear outcomes for social care [were needed] ... against which the experience of individuals can be measured and tested'. In England, the DH (2006) outlined seven national outcomes for service delivery in *Our Health, Our Care, Our Say*. More recently, the UK Coalition government consulted on outcomes frameworks for the NHS and for social care in England and Wales. While a focus on what matters to people using services might support more meaningful measures, the overall emphasis on performance continues within a managerialist paradigm. The intention here is not to argue against evaluation and accountability *per se*, but to voice caution about predominant forms. Just as there exists a more democratic citizenship-based alternative to the consumerist model of service use, so there exists an alternative, more democratic view of what performance management could be, as will be discussed in Chapter 5.

Citizenship/relationship-based approaches

In contrast with consumerist conceptualisations of the individual's interactions with services, the disability movement developed from a theoretical starting point of the social model of disability, whereby disabled people are invited to campaign collectively for their right to be full citizens (Campbell and Oliver, 1996). From this basis, the movement has sought to raise awareness of social injustices, making significant progress in campaigning for legally based rights for disabled people, resulting in various developments in anti-discrimination legislation (Barnes, 2002). However, recognition that rights, even when enshrined in legislation, do not necessarily equate with improved living conditions resulted in the emergence of the independent living movement, which has campaigned for disabled people to have the same choice and control as their non-disabled fellow citizens (Morris, 2004). There is, in fact, considerable debate within the literature as to how rights are conceptualised, including concerns about how they can be translated into practice (Drewett, 1999), about the implications for equity of self-defined need as the basis for rights claims (Handley, 2000) and whether rights-based approaches ensure justice for people with learning disabilities

(Young and Quibell, 2000; MacIntyre, 2008). Notwithstanding the importance of rights, the focus in this book is outcomes-based working and how it links to relationship-based approaches to working with disabled people.

A more user-centric conceptualisation of outcomes is represented by long-standing work on personal outcomes conducted by the Social Policy Research Unit (SPRU) at York University (Qureshi, 2001; Glendinning *et al.*, 2006) and subsequently at the University of Glasgow (Petch *et al.*, 2007) and more recently in partnership with the Scottish Government (Miller, 2010). As identified in the opening to this book, outcomes-focused services aim to achieve the aspirations, goals and priorities identified by service users. The starting point, therefore, is not to demonstrate outcomes, but to work with individuals to achieve the outcomes important to them. In this model, there are three broad sets of outcomes (Nicholas *et al.*, 2003): maintenance (with a focus on quality of life and maintaining health and well-being); change (with a focus on short-term removal of barriers to quality of life or improving health and well-being); process (with a focus on the way that services are delivered, or how the person feels they have been treated). Consistent with the policy intentions behind health and social care assessment, early evidence from SPRU suggested that an outcomes model supports: a person-centred approach, effective partnership working and best value (Nicholas *et al.*, 2003).

Discussion of the differences between needs-led and outcomes-focused approaches to working with individuals will continue in subsequent chapters, as will discussion of how outcomes interact with some of the cross-cutting themes identified in this opening chapter. Most of the remainder of this chapter will focus on partnership working and outcomes in Scotland. First, very brief consideration will be given to research on the outcomes of partnership working.

Outcomes of partnership working

The continued policy emphasis on partnership working has come under question in recent years (Petch, 2008). As with evaluation of other developments in health and social care, the tendency has been for evaluation of partnership to focus on process not outcomes (Dickinson, 2008). Most evaluations have focused on how effectively partners are working together (Hardy *et al.*, 2000). It has been argued that three levels are essential in forming effective partnerships — structural, organisation and individual — and that government has been attentive to issues of structure at the expense of organisational and individual issues (Glasby, 2003).

It can be particularly difficult to evidence benefits of partnership because the usual challenges of attribution in complex and changing systems are amplified where more than one agency is involved. Research funded under the Department of Health's Modernising Adult Social Care (MASC) initiative set out to explore the extent to which services offered in partnership between health and social care can deliver the outcomes valued by users and carers (Petch *et al.*, 2007). A fuller account is available in Chapter 2 on outcomes for service users, and features in the final section of this chapter in the section headed 'Talking Points'. The research shows good outcomes were delivered to users by the services included in the project. Although the authors conclude that there were limits to how far these could be attributed to partnership working, some key features of services relating to partnership working were identified by service users as follows.

Table 1.1: Features of partnership associated with good outcomes (Petch *et al.*, 2007).

Key features of partnership	Related features of services	Outcomes delivered
Co-location of staff	Providing a single point of contact, improving access and communication	Process outcomes, especially responsiveness Quality-of-life outcome: Feeling safe
Multi-disciplinary team	Providing holistic care	Process outcomes Quality-of-life outcomes Change outcomes
Specialist partnership	Providing specialist, non-discriminatory treatment	Process outcomes, especially being treated with respect
Extended partnership	Providing access to other agencies, and partnership with service users	Process outcome: Choice Quality-of-life outcomes, including activity and contact with other people

Partnership working, performance and outcomes in Scotland

Over the past thirteen years in Scotland, considerable effort has been invested in developing approaches to joint performance monitoring in community care. It should be noted that, although the term community care has largely been replaced with health and social care in many countries, it is still in frequent use in Scotland. For the purposes of this book, there is limited space for anything more than a very brief review of the background to relevant Scottish policy. A full account is available in another book of this series (Petch, 2008). Key policy milestones include *Modernising Community Care: An Action Plan* (Scottish Office, 1998) published five years after initial implementation of relevant sections of the 1990 NHS and Community Care Act. The aims of the action plan were to secure better and faster results for people by focusing on them and their needs; and more effective and efficient joint working based on partnership. The Joint Future Group was established by the minister for health and community care as a short-life working group to improve joint working and improve person-centred services, with early work focusing on process and structures (Petch, 2008).

The Joint Future Initiative

The Joint Future Initiative in Scotland essentially sought to establish formal partnerships between NHS boards and each of thirty-two local authorities (Forbes and Evans, 2008). (This chapter has already touched on the development of shared assessment between health and social care in each of the devolved administrations of the UK from around 2003.) Early Joint Future strategies were focused on single shared assessment as well as local partnership agreements emphasising joint resourcing and joint management. Previously, performance measures had related to single agencies. Circular CCD1/2003 introduced a new Joint Performance Information and Assessment Framework (JPIAF) seeking measures to reflect the joined-up policy agenda. The initial JPIAF formulation consisted of nine JPIAF indicators, focusing on joint management arrangements, joint resourcing and single shared assessment (SSA). Two new performance indicators were added in 2004. JPIAF Ten, introduced as a whole-systems indicator in respect of the balance of care, was to be assembled from existing data, including the number of people receiving a SSA, the number of delayed discharges, the number of over sixty-fives admitted to hospital in an emergency, the number supported in long-term care, and the number supported at home through provision of ten or more hours of home care. JPIAF Eleven sought information on outcomes for people. A consultation paper on performance measures for carers' assessments included a recommendation for indicators based on 'qualitative information on needs and outcomes preferences' (Scottish Executive, 2003, p. 29). However, given that this was not included in the short-term list of possible indicators, it was perhaps foreseeable that it was not realised.

The initial focus of the Joint Future agenda was older people, extending across community care in February 2004. Other simultaneous demands from the centre included Extended Local Partnerships Agreements to be produced by the end of April 2004, as well as plans for new structures called Community Health Partnerships and delayed discharge plans. A common observation at the time was that 'different sections within the Scottish Executive were operating within a silo mentality' (Petch, 2008, p. 76), and it is notable that housing and the voluntary sector were not included. Bruce and Forbes (2010) identify key issues including the need to define an overall vision and for more joined-up thinking at the centre, with particular criticism voiced in regard to a fixation at the centre with process over outcome.

From JPIAF towards outcomes in Scotland

From 2006 in Scotland, there was a shift in emphasis from the centre. Four national outcomes for service users and carers were identified as the objective for partnership activity, as set out in *Better Outcomes For Older People* (Scottish Executive, 2005): supporting more people at home, assisting people to lead independent lives, ensuring people receive an improved quality of care and better involvement of and support for carers. In January 2006, the Joint Future Unit circulated a letter to partnerships highlighting a variety of issues, including the importance attached to developing an outcomes approach for all client groups during the year 2006/7. A subsequent circular in 2007 signalled the intention to develop a National Outcomes Framework (NOF), including measures characterised as measuring user satisfaction with services. As with the previous performance framework, JPIAF, there was an emphasis on gathering much of the data for the measures through community care assessments. At the same time, work was underway by a practitioner manager representative group, the Assessment Review Co-ordination Group, to update the National Minimum Information Standards (NMIS) for assessment, care planning and review. The new standards were published in 2008, with references to outcomes included alongside a continued emphasis on assessment of need. Following central concerns, the primary focus was on including outcomes as measures for the new Outcomes Framework.

The national outcomes measures were specified early in 2007. These comprised four high-level outcomes — improved health, improved well-being, improved social inclusion and improved independence and responsibility — and sixteen performance measures focusing on user satisfaction with services, waiting times, quality of assessment, shifting the balance of care, carers' well-being, unscheduled care and the identification of people at risk. The measures represent more continuity than change from the previous JPIAF system.

While work was continuing on developing the National Outcomes Framework, an election returned a new Scottish Nationalist Party (SNP) government to Scotland's Parliament. Shortly afterwards, the publication of the *Concordat* (Scottish Government, 2007b) set out the terms of a new relationship between central and local government with the funding to be provided to local government to be reduced from eighty funding streams to fifteen and a new single reporting system, the Single Outcome Agreement (SOA), to replace the myriad existing systems. For the key areas of activity that take place in health and social care in the thirty-two partnerships across Scotland, the SOA is now the over-arching tool for reporting how services are delivering outcomes for service users and carers across Scotland, albeit at a strategic level (Gooday and Stewart, 2009, p. 32). Given the 'new relationship' signalled by the *Concordat*, it was no longer possible for the centre to impose a uniform performance framework on local partnerships. Therefore the National Outcomes Framework was renamed the Community Care Outcomes Framework, with the understanding that this would operate at the discretion of local partnerships and 'below the waterline' of the mandatory reporting framework of the SOA. These developments are summarised in Table 1.2.

Table 1.2: Outcomes related developments influencing community care.

Policy development	Description	Level of implementation
Talking Points: Personal Outcomes Approach (Cook *et al.*, 2007)	Approach to implementing outcomes-based working with all agencies involved in assessment and delivery of health and social care services	Almost all local authorities to varying extents, including all early implementers, some health organisations and increasing numbers of independent sector providers
Community Care Outcomes Framework (Scottish Executive, 2007a)	Performance management framework for community care, consists of sixteen measures, four outcomes and the rest outputs and processes	At early 2011, all local authority partnerships are members of the Community Care Benchmarking Network. Most have implemented some measures, especially those consistent with NHS HEAT targets
Single Outcome Agreement, brought in with *Concordat* (Scottish Government, 2007b)	High-level outcomes reporting between central and local government	All local authorities with key partners — mandatory — with space for local priorities and reporting arrangements
National Minimum Information Standards (Scottish Government, 2008)	Information standards for assessment, care planning and review and carer assessment, to be implemented flexibly by partnerships, and including four outcomes measures relating to the CCOF	All local authorities with varying degrees of involvement of health partners, but without the formal government compliance process, which had been in place previously

Talking Points: Personal outcomes approach

In 2006, a separate but related development was initiated by the Joint Improvement Team (JIT) of the Scottish Government. The JIT was established in 2004 on the basis of a recommendation from the Joint Future Implementation and Advisory Group, with a view to creating a specialist team to work with health and social care partnerships to accelerate delivery of service improvements for service users and carers (Petch, 2008). The team is a partnership body, funded by the government, NHS Scotland and the Convention of Scottish Local Authorities (COSLA).

In spring 2006, the assistant director of the JIT commissioned the researchers who had undertaken the work on the MASC project. They were to develop an approach to implementing service user and carer outcomes in community care in Scotland. This work started on a small scale in 2006 through recruiting local partnerships to take part in testing out the feasibility of building outcomes into individual reviews. Positive results in engaging with people using services were reported from staff and managers involved, as well as in relation to the usefulness of the outcomes data gathered from users and carers. These initial findings and the tools used were collated into a report, which was made available to local partnerships (Cook *et al.*, 2007). During this early stage of the development work, the overall approach was known as the UDSET (User Defined Service Evaluation Toolkit).

What subsequently came to be known as the Talking Points approach has continued to grow and develop through a long-term knowledge exchange partnership between the researchers, the Joint Improvement Team and representatives from community care organisations across Scotland. Similar to the approach adapted by SPRU, Talking Points seeks to maximise outcomes for users of community care services and their unpaid carers as follows:

- by focusing on outcomes in interactions with people using services and their unpaid carers, including finding out from individuals what is most important to them in life and identifying how everyone can work together to achieve the best outcomes possible for that person. The information gathered can be recorded in outcomes-focused support plans. The circumstances of the person can be revisited at review, including checking out whether outcomes are being achieved;
- by using information on service user and carer outcomes captured during these interactions to support service improvement and the planning and commissioning of services and performance management.

When work started on developing UDSET in 2006, it was initially viewed as a short-term piece of work with the objective of developing a toolkit to measure personal outcomes in community care. As the work progressed on an incremental basis, however, it emerged that genuinely focusing on user and carer outcomes in fact requires not only significant investment in changing the culture and processes within a service but also wider reorientation of systems. The work has extended more recently to involve other agencies including the voluntary sector and the independent care-home and care-at-home sectors. It has developed into a large-scale change management programme which has attempted both to respond to policy developments and to shape them. For example, a range of government strategies which emerged in 2010 reference Talking Points and/or Talking Points outcomes, with numerous references in the carers' strategy, dementia strategy and self-directed support strategy as well as a reference in the NHS quality strategy.

Conclusion

This chapter has explored the recent context to health and social care policy in the UK. This included consideration of the postwar development of the welfare state and some of the structural and cultural tensions which were built in from the outset. It has identified continuing key challenges which have beset the development of community care, including the challenges of working across agency boundaries, a long-standing trend of underfunding of the community sector, and differences between the medical and social models, including varying levels of paternalism across services. Many of the tensions described cannot be defined simplistically as between health and social care, because they are also partly influenced on the health side by whether the service in question is community or hospital based.

The 1990 NHS and Community Care Act is highlighted as representing a watershed in the history of community care. The Act was ostensibly introduced to address some of the issues identified, and to make assessment of need a cornerstone of the system, linked to identification of care packages. An inherent tension, however, continuing in policy to the present, is the focus on consumerisation in parallel with cost containment. The reality is that the complexity of community care has increased with marketisation, managerialism and the introduction of many new partners in social care in particular. And as the system becomes more complex, the person who requires support moves further away from the centre to a remote location on the periphery of the system and policy.

Two competing paradigms are highlighted to try to make sense of the enduring nature of the contradictions in the system: the New Right/managerialist and the relationship/outcomes-based approach.

It is possible to identify a range of initiatives over the years since the 1990 Act which emerge from one or other paradigm, or a combination of both. A key challenge in assessing the merits of initiatives is that the New Right has increasingly presented its policies using progressive language claiming to meet consumer demand and empower the individual (Brodie *et al.*, 2008). Opposition to such proposals is easily made to appear reactive and passive (Clarke and Newman, 1997).

The approach to outcomes-based working which has developed in Scotland has emerged from a relationship-based approach, but has at times sat uneasily between the two paradigms. In some senses, it could also be justifiably argued that outcomes-based working is a restricted form of democratic involvement because it does not inherently include a focus on direct user representation at the strategic level of organisations. Whilst acknowledging that limitation, it is also important to emphasise the very significant challenges involved in trying to locate user and carer priorities at the centre of a managerialist system, with a range of pressures brought to bear to prioritise consumerist and performance agendas at the risk of eclipsing the improving potential of outcomes-based working. Through exploring the outcomes approach from the various perspectives involved, the intention is to highlight potential benefits and pitfalls with recommendations for policy and practice.

CHAPTER 2

Outcomes for People Who Use Health and Social Care Services

> I was a bit apprehensive when I knew there would be four young women. I call them 'my girls'. It was just what kind of girls they would be. I had friends who had care and it seemed to be a bossy girl. It was what they said — not what you wanted. And I couldna have coped with that. I really couldna. I very quickly realised that they were there to do the work, but to have a laugh as well. It was just a very, very comfortable arrangement. (Service user 'My Girls' digital story on the JIT website)

This chapter will start by exploring the evidence about what matters to people using community care services, and particularly the outcomes identified as important, including differences between groups of users. Chapter 1 touched on earlier research on personal outcomes by SPRU at the University of York, and on more recent research undertaken at the University of Glasgow, as part of the wider Department of Health MASC research programme. In Chapter 2 the focus is the findings on outcomes. One of the key learning points from the work was the level of continuity of the outcomes that matter to people.

On the basis of the research findings, an approach to outcomes-based working has been developed in community care in Scotland. This has progressed with continuing reference to the earlier work by SPRU in England, and in correspondence with contemporary work in Wales. In keeping with the two paradigms outlined in the first chapter, Chapter 2 will consider outcomes-based working in the context of the consumerist paradigm. This will include developments in personalisation in the UK, alongside recent policy espousing more enabling relationships between services and users and carers, based on conceptualisations of citizenship and reciprocity.

A range of terms is currently in use to describe people who use health and social care services, denoting both the perceptions of staff in different services as well as the different paradigms in operation. They include patient, service user, client, consumer and customer. Although less than ideal to define an individual by their use of services, 'service user' is the main term used in this book in the absence of an ideal alternative.

MASC outcomes research project

This chapter will begin by considering the objectives, methods and particularly the findings of the research project which set out to redress the paucity of evidence on partnership working, by investigating the outcomes for service users. For the purposes of this book, it is the findings about outcomes *per se* which are of most relevance as these formed the basis of the subsequent programme of work in Scotland. The full report on the research is available on the Joint Improvement Team website (Petch *et al.,* 2007). To summarise, the project sought to meet the overall aim of identifying outcomes of partnership working by addressing the following research objectives:

- to determine the outcomes that service users want from services;
- to assess the extent to which health and social care partnerships deliver the outcomes that service users value;
- to determine the features of partnership working that deliver these outcomes;
- to refine the initial interview schedule into a generic user-defined service effectiveness tool.

These objectives were explored in the context of fifteen health and social care partnerships supporting older people, individuals with mental health problems or with learning disabilities. The research was conducted in partnership with three user-led organisations — Service User Research Enterprise, Central England People First and Older People Researching Social Issues — representing the three user groups who would be interviewed about the outcomes of partnership working. In order to address the first aim of the project, identifying the outcomes important to service users, the starting point was to revisit work on social care outcomes developed by SPRU (Qureshi, 2001), which conceptualised the most important outcomes for users of social care services as falling into three categories:

- maintenance (quality of life);
- change (recovery and removing barriers to quality of life);
- process (how people are treated by services).

In the early stages of the MASC project, the validity of these outcomes was explored during three focus groups involving our service-user research partners. Key concerns in this process were ensuring that the original work by SPRU, which was largely based on work with older people and focused on social care, was applicable to a wider range of service users and a broader range of services, using language understandable to people with diverse needs.

The core common outcomes which emerged as being important from the focus groups with different user groups are detailed in Table 2.1. This table of outcomes is similar in many respects to those identified in the research by SPRU (Qureshi and Nicholas, 2001). The key difference in the remaining outcomes is in the use of language, as our service-user research colleagues identified language that made sense to individuals using a variety of services.

Table 2.1: Outcomes important to people who use services

Quality of life	Process	Change
Feeling safe	Listened to	Improved confidence and skills
Having things to do	Choice	Improved mobility
Seeing people	Treated as an individual	Reduced symptoms
Staying well	Reliability	
Living life as you want	Responsiveness	
Living where you want		
Dealing with stigma/ discrimination		

Following from the focus groups, an interview schedule was developed based on a revised set of outcomes (Petch *et al.,* 2005) and divided into four sections: the help you get; how using the service impacts on you and your life; what happens when you use the service; and, finally, your thoughts on the service overall. This questionnaire was included in the early version of the toolkit which was developed with the subsequent knowledge exchange programme with the JIT (Cook *et al.*, 2007).

The next phase required identification of partnerships to involve, including five for each group of service users. A mapping process had highlighted the diversity and complexity of partnerships operating in the field. As distinct models of partnership were not discernible on the ground, it was not possible to set up the research in such a way that we could deduce that one model of partnership was more effective than another. This shaped the sampling strategy to focus at the level of specific services delivered in partnership, as this was where service users were most likely to notice any difference that partnership working made. Interviews were conducted with 230 individuals across the fifteen partnerships. Most of the interviews lasted between thirty and ninety minutes. Paid and unpaid carers acted as proxies for service users in a small number of the interviews involving people with severe learning disabilities.

The data gathered in the interviews was used to identify where and how outcomes were delivered by the partnerships. We then considered which partnership features supported delivery of the outcomes described, as shown in Table 1.2.

Research findings on outcomes across care groups
There were sufficient numbers of interviews involved to be able to identify patterns in the responses (Petch *et al.*, 2007). Perhaps most significantly, all outcomes were found to be salient to all user groups. The outcomes most relevant to respondents from all groups were having things to do and contact with other people. Some interviewees from all three groups indicated that how they were treated by staff could be as important as what services achieved with regard to quality of life and change outcomes. It should be noted that the emphasis in this research was on evaluation of services and therefore on outcomes attributable to services, rather than in respect of the person's whole life. This means that many of the differences identified from the research relate to the routes into and patterns of service use as experienced by each group. The most prevalent themes for each user group are set out in Table 2.2.

Table 2.2: Outcomes across care groups

Outcome	Older people	Mental health	Learning disabilities
Quality of life			
Feeling safe	Knowing someone is there to keep an eye on the person = proactive monitoring Fear of crime in the neighbourhood Fear of falling	Knowing support is available should a crisis occur Fear of discrimination and stigma	Knowing there is someone trusted to talk to in case of crisis or distress Fear of harassment in the neighbourhood or from other service users
Having things to do	Getting out and about Availability of activities valued	Opportunities for employment and other meaningful activities	Choice of activities including physical and recreational Employment opportunities
Contact with other people	Social isolation very common. Home care often the sole form of social contact Groups valued by many (more often by females)	Social contact with other users particularly valued. Opportunities to socialise in a stigma-free environment emphasised	Social contact with staff particularly valued Social contact with other users appreciated Establishing relationships in the community challenging
Staying as well as you can be	Access to a range of professionals often important in recovering from health crises. Combating social isolation important to sustain health	Access to support both preventatively and in the longer term if required, rather than restricted to crisis times.	Role of staff in supporting access to mainstream and specialist health services
Process			
Being listened to	Having a say in services	Having a say in services	Having a say in services
Feeling valued and treated with respect	Not being patronised Treated as an individual	Staff seeing beyond the label	Not being patronised
Having choices	Choice over timing of services and tasks undertaken Access to information about services	Choice over treatment options important Choice of activities appreciated Choice of accommodation often restricted	Choice of activities emphasised Choice over where people lived and who with important
Having people to rely on	Staff turning up and on time often problematic, particularly in relation to home care. Communication important in such cases	Knowing that staff would turn up important and a phone call to inform of changed arrangements appreciated	Knowing that staff would turn up important and a phone call to inform of changed arrangements appreciated
Knowing someone will respond	Ability to contact someone and rely on a quick response in a crisis	Ability to contact someone and rely on a quick response in a crisis	Ability to contact someone and rely on a quick response in a crisis
Change			
Improving skills and confidence	Most older people using partnership services had experienced health crisis and emphasised the role of services in restoring skills and confidence	Support with re-establishing skills and confidence following hospitalisation	Where periods of ill health had occurred, the role of services in restoring skills and confidence was valued
Improving mobility	Restoring ability to walk where possible and/or supply of adaptations where necessary.	Support to use public transport	Availability of transport Support to use transport
Reducing symptoms	Reducing pain and discomfort Reducing symptoms of mental illness where required	Reducing and/or managing anxiety, depression and other aspects of mental illness	Reducing pain and discomfort Reducing symptoms of mental illness where required

Some caveats can be applied to these findings. First is that these findings fail to take into account that many people cut across (service-led) categorisations according to care group. This type of categorisation in practice results in individuals falling into gaps between services. Secondly, we found that there were as many differences within groups as between them. However, taking these reservations into account, there were discernible differences in factors associated with different outcomes according to user group. This is not inherently related to the person's condition or disability. Consistent with the social model of disability, many of the distinctions relate to societal responses to disability, or the way that services are provided. To take the example of stigma/discrimination first, stigma was a concept which was particularly familiar to people using mental health services. The importance of having a safe place to mix with others who they could trust would not judge or fear them, because of their mental illness, was frequently highlighted. When discussing discrimination, several people with learning disabilities described incidents of being bullied or intimidated by members of the public. Older people viewed the treatment they received in the acute sector unfavourably when compared to the generally more positive way they were treated by staff in their community-based partnership service.

Contact and relationships with staff were viewed differently according to care group. A reliance on staff as key social contacts was more apparent amongst people with learning disabilities, several of whom emphasised the importance of one-to-one time, and being able to confide in a member of staff. People using mental health services were less likely to highlight relationships with staff, although some people did identify individual members of staff who played an important role in keeping them well. Mental health service users more often emphasised the role of peer support in forming trusted relationships with others, influenced by concerns about being stigmatised. Whereas it was apparent from the interviews that many people with learning disabilities and users of mental health services did not feel fully included in society, many older people were sufficiently isolated that any contact with other people was welcomed. Some identified the human contact aspect of home care as what

mattered most to them, with many identifying that knowing some-
one would keep an eye on them was critical to feeling safe.

It is not possible to discuss all the outcomes covered in the research.
Considering individual stories, it was often clear that change outcomes were directly linked to quality-of-life outcomes and in turn
the relationship with staff or one key member of staff was identified as having played a critical role either in restoring or maintaining well-being. Being able to understand how outcomes interact has
implications for evidencing and understanding how support is best
organised.

A number of barriers and supports to delivering good outcomes
were identified. The key barriers did not necessarily relate specifically
to partnership but to services more generally. This is consistent with
findings of other projects which try to assess the impacts of policy
on the ground, with service users just as likely to describe the impact
of funding restrictions as that of improvements in service design
(Newman, 2005). Identified barriers were:

- staffing levels and continuity of staffing;
- limits to resources;
- access to transport particularly in rural areas;
- time-limited services (e.g. intermediate care services limited
  to six weeks).

What emerged from this project was that evaluation based on the
outcomes important to service users provides rich data about the
impact of services on the ground. Although it is not always possible
to identify which aspect of a service delivers an identified outcome,
some service users, encouraged by a good exchange with an inter-
viewer, can comment on these connections. Furthermore, analysis
of patterns emerging from data yielded by a relatively small number
of interviews in one partnership can identify barriers and supports
to delivery of outcomes (Petch *et al.*, 2007).

Although we interviewed service managers in order to identify
structural and procedural aspects of partnership arrangements, we
did not include staff perspectives. While the purpose of the research
was to investigate outcomes for users, in retrospect the inclusion of
staff perspectives might have supported a fuller understanding of
pressures and opportunities at the front line, influencing outcomes

for service users. The incorporation of staff perspectives has proven essential in the subsequent development of outcomes-based working, as will be discussed in Chapter 4 in particular.

From research to practice: Developing outcomes-based working in Scotland

A programme of work initiating development of an outcomes focus in community care began in 2006, when the assistant director of the JIT commissioned the researchers involved in the MASC research at the University of Glasgow to work with partnerships in Scotland to develop a toolkit to take this forward. While the opening section of this chapter focused directly on outcomes for service users, the next section will identify some of the barriers identified by staff to implementing outcomes-based working.

The work on outcomes began with two workshops, which included representatives from a range of health and social care partnerships. The findings of the research on outcomes were presented at these events, and local areas were invited to participate in piloting of outcomes work. Small-scale pilots were subsequently set up in three areas: Orkney, Fife and East Renfrewshire. The results of these pilots are reported in the original UDSET report (Cook *et al.*, 2007). Following from the early piloting work, there was an increased interest at a national level, as the Community Care Outcomes Framework emerged. Seven local authority area partnerships signed up as early implementers of the outcomes framework, each selecting a range of measures to work on. All but one of the early implementers volunteered to test out what was still the UDSET at that time. Key findings from this stage of development are included in the evaluation undertaken by Glasgow School of Social Work (Stewart, 2008).

A reality check

When the work began in 2006, the expectation was that the outcomes be transferred into assessment tools and this would form a basis for improved involvement of service users. A second assumption was that building outcomes into assessment tools would refocus performance management around outcomes. The more complex reality of such a significant change management agenda emerged quickly, as a range of issues were identified by practitioners which needed to be addressed to make outcomes-based working a reality. In retrospect, the work at this stage encountered the two key 'gaps' identified by the Cooksey Report (2006) on the facilitation of research into practice: namely, the translation of research into new products and approaches; and the implementation of new approaches into practice. It quickly became clear that, rather than a simplistic transfer of knowledge from research to practice, the programme would need to be based on a model of knowledge exchange, involving the researchers, the JIT and other policy colleagues, and partnerships and agencies across Scotland, who in turn involved service users and carers in a range of ways in different localities.

An early example of an issue highlighted by practitioners was the need to identify and implement an outcomes framework for carers, particularly given the critical role of unpaid carers in supporting health and social care services. One of the earliest objectives identified for the programme, therefore, was to develop a separate outcomes framework for carers, so that distinct tools for service users and carers could be incorporated into the toolkit. The details of that work will be described in further detail in Chapter 3.

A second example was the challenge to integrate an outcomes focus into a wider system which was explicitly deficit focused and to a large extent service led. Single Shared Assessment in particular was identified as a barrier. This is consistent with previous research by Glendinning *et al.* (2006) who identify shared assessment in England as a barrier to achieving outcomes-focused services for older people. Work was therefore initiated with staff, in attempting to understand training and organisational development requirements to make the shift towards focusing on outcomes in assessment, planning and review, as will be discussed in Chapter 4.

A further systems-based barrier which was highlighted by staff was the need for outcomes-focused planning and commissioning of services. While many staff welcomed the opportunity to conduct outcomes-focused conversations with service users, they were concerned that existing services, particularly those focused on tasks and outputs, were not conducive to outcomes. Work on these themes and associated outputs are described in Chapters 4 and 5.

In the context of wider discussions about performance management and outcomes, which will continue throughout this book, it is
important to note that a tension soon emerged. While the initial focus
was using service-user outcomes as a basis for evaluating services,
this quickly shifted. The outcomes research for the MASC project
had demonstrated that it is possible to undertake one-off evaluation
exercises based on the outcomes that matter to individuals. However,
in more routine practice, an evaluation focus at the review stage only
can miss the point of outcomes-based working. Practitioners quickly
realised that simply reviewing outcomes for individuals did not make
sense. They were undertaking reviews with service users on a different
basis from which they had been assessed. Outcomes-based working
involves having a different kind of conversation, which should not
start from a service focus. A qualitative conversation at an early stage
of engagement offered potential to move from a service-led, deficit-
focused approach to assessment to a more enabling, strengths-based
approach, through more actively involving the individual in identifying their outcomes and how they might be achieved. This shift
will be explained further in Chapters 3 and 4. The key early shift in
understanding can be summarised as follows:

Table 2.3: Moving from UDSET to Talking Points: Developing an understanding of
outcomes-based working

U	User Defined	Users and carers have distinct outcomes, which both need to be considered, therefore two separate frameworks of outcomes involved	**Talking**
D	Service	Focusing on outcomes means engaging with the person in the context of their whole life, not just through the filter of the services they fit into	**Points:**
S	Evaluation	Focus on service evaluation alone too often ignores the contribution the person makes to their outcomes, missing the enablement potential of outcomes-based working	**Personal-**
E			**outcomes**
T	Toolkit	There has been excessive attention to filling in assess-ment tools, and box ticking. A challenge is to restore staff communication, relationship building and analytical skills	**approach**

A further challenge in moving towards outcomes-based working
concerns public expectations of what services do. If an individual
has a history of service use which has led them to expect services
to do things to and make decisions for them, it can be as much of a

challenge for that person to begin thinking about a more active role in both defining and working towards their outcomes, as it can be for staff. Therefore, many of the support materials which have been developed to support culture change towards outcomes-based working, including a range of digital stories and case studies, have been designed for use with audiences including service users and carers.

Communication

A further key issue raised by staff in the early stages, and repeatedly identified as important by users and carers, is to ensure that service users with communication support needs are not excluded from outcomes-based assessment. Initially, staff expressed concern that there were risks of creating a two-tier system. Work on developing material to support this issue began in 2008, to ensure that individuals with cognitive impairments/ communication difficulties could be included. This has involved collaborative work between the originators of a low-tech symbolic communication support tool called Talking Mats (Murphy *et al.*, 2010), the Talking Points team and staff from various organisations. This resulted in a set of symbols in many ways similar to those generally used in Talking Mats, but matched to the Talking Points outcomes. While no one communication aid will suit all individuals, initial responses from staff using the symbols with all care groups were very positive. Further to this, it also became clear that there were other barriers to effective communication for practitioners who had worked within assessment processes which were often tightly prescribed and very service focused, as will be discussed in Chapter 4.

Having discussed some of the key challenges and strategies to achieving outcomes-based working with service users in Scotland, this chapter will consider parallel developments in choice and personalisation, and how they interact with outcomes.

The consumerist paradigm: Choice in health and social care services

The opening chapter included reference to the introduction of monetarist policies in the UK in the 1980s. Central to this version of monetarism was public choice theory, which has influenced a succession of UK governments. During the period that the MASC research was being conducted, there was a renewed emphasis from the New Labour government on the importance of 'choice' in public services, with a particular focus on the NHS in England. Fitting with a neoliberal conceptualisation of public consumption of services, the problem with public services is identified as paternalism, which is associated with monopoly provision by the public sector. The solution, therefore, was to introduce contestability and choice by opening up the market. Picking up on concerns about the impact of marketisation on health inequalities, the argument also makes claims about choice and equity:

> Choice mechanisms enhance equity by exerting pressure on low-quality or incompetent providers. Competitive pressures and incentives drive up quality, efficiency and responsiveness in the public sector. Choice leads to higher standards. The overriding principle is clear. We should give poorer patients the same range of choice the rich have always enjoyed (Blair, 2003).

The question of whether marketisation can in itself improve service quality will be discussed below. Before that, conceptualisation of choice merits consideration because of discrepancies between the predominant policy emphasis and what service users identify as important. Although the outcome of 'choice' was included in the MASC project research schedule, it is notable that not one of 230 interviewees identified choice between services as a priority. Instead, individuals repeatedly identified that having a say in how and when services were delivered was what mattered to them. Far more often, relationships and meaningful activity were identified as supporting well-being. Indeed, it has been repeatedly demonstrated by other research projects that relationships with service providers at every level of service delivery matter more than choice between providers (Bell and Smerdon, 2011).

There is a broad-based acceptance that paternalism in public services needs to be challenged where it prevails (Clarke and Newman, 1997) and that more inclusive ways of working with the public will support the sustainability of services (Boyle and Harris, 2009). It is the means of achieving this culture shift which is contested. The limits of choice/contestability as a vehicle for delivering person-centred care and support can be illustrated by consideration of one of the sectors opened to the market earliest, following the 1990 Act, namely home care. Home care provision became progressively more focused on those identified as most at need for many years after 1990, to the extent that the proportion of older people receiving home care in England was identified as low by international standards (CSCI, 2006). Research by Bauld *et al.* (2000) compared provision of home care before and after the 1990 Act and found that more targeted intensive care packages had resulted in supporting people to stay at home. However, this was at the expense of withdrawing low-level, preventative support services. Marketisation was accompanied by a shift in priorities so that key quality-of-life outcomes were redefined as insufficiently significant to merit support. Lack of preventive support, however, can present risks to physical and mental well-being, in turn reducing the ability of older people to remain at home (Means *et al.*, 2008).

So there are limits to choice at the outset with regard to individuals being able to access services, and further limits for those who get through the gatekeeping processes. The development of markets in the home care sector has not in itself succeeded in delivering meaningful choice to individuals, or the quality, efficiency and responsiveness referred to by Blair. While an increase in provider numbers does not necessarily translate into better choices for people, there is potential for improvement through outcomes-focused commissioning and the development of a more enabling culture. The case of home care will be revisited in Chapter 5, in considering organisational imperatives and alternative approaches.

Personalisation

This chapter will conclude by considering developments around the personalisation agenda, and implications for outcomes-based working. The concept of personalisation has been a key theme in health and social care for several years. In its broadest formulation, personalisation advocates a tailored response to individual circumstances rather than standardised off-the-peg solutions. Increasingly, however, personalisation has come to be equated with self-directed support. Self-directed support describes a range of mechanisms which give service users control over a budget allocated to them for support services, affording choice about how the budget should be spent (Cook, 2008). Direct payments were the original means of delivering self-directed support, whereby individuals were given cash to employ a personal assistant or to purchase services from their chosen provider. More recently, other options identified include the nomination of a third party to administer the budget on behalf of the individual, or the continued involvement of a care manager in supporting the individual to purchase their care. At the core of self-directed support is the involvement of the user in defining their needs/outcomes in a plan, the calculation of an upfront budget to meet those needs/outcomes, and then various degrees of user control in determining the spend of the budget. One of the key agencies promoting personalisation has been the thinktank Demos. The market orientation of their ethos is evident in the report *Personalisation through Participation* in which they argue that 'personalisation could have a similar impact and reach' as privatisation (Leadbetter, 2004, p. 18). Concern has been expressed recently about the increasing consumerist/managerialist emphasis in the implementation of self-directed support (Beresford, 2008).

Previously, direct payment or independent living schemes were legal only if social services gave a grant for a third party to run such schemes on behalf of others (Means *et al.*, 2008). The Community Care (Direct Payments) Act 1996 gave physically disabled people and people with learning disabilities, below the age of sixty-five, the possibility of receiving a payment to arrange their own care services. The private member's bill was advocated by the British Council of Organisations of Disabled People and the Independent Living Movement to enable people to employ their own staff and manage their own care. Direct payments were extended to older people by the Labour government from February 2000.

There has been some variation in approaches to personalisation in the devolved administrations of the UK, centring on the extent to which the market is promoted as the means for delivery of the elusive policy goal of achieving person-centred support. In the late 1990s, the

New Labour government outlined the 'third way for social care' in the White Paper *Modernising Adult Social Care Services* (DH, 1998). Delivering a boost to the market, this Paper asserted that the agency providing care was less important than the quality of care. Although the themes of choice and control were emphasised, a more pressing influence remained the spiralling costs of care provision (Means *et al.*, 2008), which remains a driver behind personalisation policy. Ten years later, in the context of intensified concerns about costs, *Putting People First* (DH, 2008) placed notions of choice and control, associated largely with self-directed support, centre stage in England. Local authority performance indicator NI130 required that by April 2011 30% of all community-based services were to be delivered as a direct payment or personal budget. Although the target required evidence that the person exercised choice in constructing their care plan, it did not require that the person be given any choice about having such a personal budget in the first place (Clements, 2011).

In Scotland, the twenty-first century review of social work (*Changing Lives*) was underpinned by the aspiration to create personalisation through participation for service users 'helping them achieve personal goals and aspirations' (Scottish Executive, 2006, p. 9). Outcomes-based working fits well with this broad conceptualisation of personalisation. While self-directed support may provide a possible route to achieving individual outcomes, it is only one of a range of options. Since *Changing Lives*, there has been an increasing emphasis on self-directed support in Scotland. New national guidance on self-directed support was published in 2007 (Scottish Executive, 2007b), aiming to increase uptake. The 2007 guidance in Scotland identified various supports for local authorities to fund in order to ensure effective implementation of self-directed support (MacIntyre, 2008):

- a local support service which, where possible, should be independent and user led;
- early involvement of individuals with the local support service to assist with self-assessment and care planning;
- other essential training for individuals on self-directed support, and training of personal assistants (PAs);
- all basic costs within a PA employer's package where appropriate;

- designated self-directed support lead officers or teams within each local authority;
- training on self-directed support for care managers, finance managers and local authority directors;
- enhanced disclosure for PAs employed by individuals on self-directed support.

These resource requirements are considerable, particularly in the economic climate in which personalisation is being implemented. This is particularly important given the emphasis on risk enablement associated with personalisation. Risk enablement needs to be balanced with safeguarding to avoid unnecessary harm (Carr, 2010), which implies that some of the cost-cutting motivations behind self-directed support need to be treated with caution. At the time of writing, consideration is being given in Scotland to creating enabling legislation to make self-directed support the default position for adult social care.

Wales has taken a distinct approach to personalisation, as evidenced in its recent social care White Paper, which emphasises the need to refocus on relationships and interdependence and takes a broad view of 'personalisation' (Welsh Assembly, 2011):

> 3.16 We believe that the label 'personalisation' has become too closely associated with a market-led model of consumer choice, but we are taken by the Commission's approach to stronger citizen control. We will therefore expect our recently published guidance on commissioning to drive services built on this approach.

Conclusion

A key objective of the MASC research described in this chapter was to investigate the outcomes of partnership working from service user perspectives. This chapter has highlighted findings from the research on the outcomes important to people who use a range of community care services, as well as some differences in emphases between user groups and the interplay between different types of outcomes. While the findings on outcomes specifically from partnership were perhaps less significant, this does not necessarily mean that partnership working is not beneficial to service users. In certain respects, it is easier to evidence negative outcomes for users associated with lack of partnership working. In addition, as Dickinson (2008) argues, lack of partnership has been shown repeatedly to result in serious harm being caused to individuals. Services need to work together because people do not live their lives according to the categories the care systems have created. Real-life problems are nearly always harder to define and more difficult to resolve than one service can manage.

In developing and implementing an outcomes-focused approach over the past few years in Scotland, the focus has been on knowledge exchange — in understanding staff and organisational perspectives, identifying barriers to implementation and working with colleagues on the front line to overcome those barriers. This has involved engaging with the complex world within which services operate, and it has been challenging at times to retain a focus on the people using those services. The extent to which service users and carers have been involved directly in implementing outcomes-based working has varied across localities. More often, information on outcomes from a user and carer perspective has been used for performance, planning and commissioning purposes, which will be discussed further in Chapter 5.

Research on outcomes informs about what is important to people and outcomes-based practice brings us back to that point, despite the complications in people's lives, in the system and between agencies. Consumerist conceptualisations of people who use services, centred around the politically defined interpretation of choice as contestability, are presented as alternatives to paternalism in public services. However, being able to choose between services is not a priority for service users, and marketisation in itself does not necessarily result in improved quality or responsiveness. Outcomes-based working offers an alternative to market-oriented solutions. However, the potential of outcomes to improve services does depend on organisational values and policy context, which will also be discussed in Chapter 5.

CHAPTER 3

Carers as Partners

> I felt as if we were sitting round the table having a conversation. She started asking me questions in a different way, to make me look at my life and to look at what I was not doing. Not what I *was* doing, what I was *not* doing. It took this carer's assessment to see things in black and white. (Carer, 'Black and White' digital story on the JIT website)

This chapter will begin by discussing why a separate chapter on carers was viewed as necessary, before moving on to consider some of the challenges around defining carers and the recent history of caring as a public policy issue, which some have characterised as policy opportunism (Cavaye, 2006). Consideration will then be given to outcomes for and partnership with unpaid carers. The inclusion of carers as key partners has been identified as a critical component of outcomes-based working, and focusing on outcomes as a precondition for effective partnership with carers. Carers' assessment is a key issue, and will be considered in this chapter as representing both a barrier and potential for progress in partnership working with carers.

Why a separate chapter about carers?

Reviewing literature on community care, it is evident that service users and carers are often referred to as one group. Indeed, several authors caution against separation of users and carers, including other contributors to this series (McPhail, 2008; MacIntyre, 2008). There are good reasons for this caution, including the risks of creating a false dichotomy between carer and cared for, particularly as many disabled people are also actively involved in caring roles (Morris, 1993). Informal caring takes place within a relationship which is likely to be mutual and reciprocal (Lloyd, 2001) rather than based on unidirectional roles of giver and receiver of care. There can also be a tendency for carers' voices to be privileged over the voices of cared-for people as virtuously active agents as compared to users of resources (Harris, 2002). A further issue that would support the case for maintaining the links between carer and cared for is that the 'pecking order' of conditions, or judgements about relative worthiness, have been found to apply to carers as well as service users. The *Caring with Confidence* programme (DH, 2009) identified four categories of carer, each encountering different societal attitudes. Where the condition of the person cared for could be categorised as a classic medical condition or part of the 'natural order', the experience of the carer was that they were viewed more sympathetically and were more able to accept their situation. With mental illness, carers tended to find their situation more challenging, and with more nebulous conditions such as Attention Deficit Hyperactivity Disorder (ADHD) or Myalgic Encephalomyelitis (ME) carers found it difficult to prove their situation valid, sometimes with serious effects on self-esteem.

Given these concerns, it might be argued that service users and carers' perspectives should be covered in one chapter. However, there are two reasons for having a separate chapter in this book. The first reason is that carers' outcomes are different, because of the specific role that they play in the system. The second reason is partly related to that. While we have already discussed the enduring limitations of delivering on policy intentions to involve service users more effectively in health and social care services, there are further specific hurdles faced by carers. Supporting unpaid carers is essential to the success of community care, and this is recognised in policy (Aldred and Gott, 2005; Cavaye, 2006; Jarvis, 2010). Carers' assessments have been promoted as a key means of identifying the needs of carers, and promoted at policy level as the initial step to accessing support and services for carers. However, although increasing uptake of carer assessment has been a long-standing goal for community care, there remains a 'considerable and enduring gap between policy and practice' (Seddon *et al.*, 2006, p. 1335) centring round the ambiguous role of carers, with doubts remaining about their legitimacy as recipients of support in their own right, and continuing failure to recognise their knowledge and expertise about the cared-for person. As the population of unpaid carers increases, along with the intensity of caring, it is imperative that services work with carers to provide the information and support they require, and that carers are treated as partners (Hanson *et al.*, 2006).

Definitions of caring

The ambiguous position of carers is signalled by definitional complexity, with the question of what defines a carer challenging to resolve. A search for clarity can be viewed as unhelpful in some respects, because fixed definitions can create a false impression that individuals involved in the health and social care world have static roles, either 'service user', 'carer' or 'professional' (McPhail, 2008), belying the fact that is not unusual for a person to move between these roles at different stages of their lives.

In a similar vein, the terms 'care' and 'dependency' have contested meanings. With regard to the notion of dependency of older people in particular, earlier work by Townsend (1981) usefully questioned the tendency towards structured dependency of old age, or dependency fostered and imposed by society. Around the same time, feminist critiques questioned assumptions equating traditional female roles with unpaid care of older people (Ungerson, 1987). Indeed, as evidenced in Chapter 1, assumptions were made about the role of female care providers in the domestic sphere as the welfare state emerged. Feminists and disability writers have highlighted the concept of interdependence as being more useful. More recent work by Fine and Glendinning (2005) argues for a more positive evaluation of care and dependency, to allow individuals to develop their capabilities:

> to effect meaningful changes in their own lives, to manage the inevitable dependencies of life and to reduce or eliminate secondary, socially-imposed dependencies that deny their attainment of autonomy — 'in the systems of nested dependencies that constitute the broader system of relationships of care.' (Fine and Glendinning, 2005, p. 616)

Also related to dependency within caring relationships are notions of power and control. In her research with hidden carers, Cavaye (2006) found that control of caregiving situations could be complicated, sometimes established through ownership of material resources. A widely held belief amongst caregivers, whether resident with the cared-for person or not, was that homeownership and control of financial resources conferred a degree of authority that enabled the homeowner to control the situation. Other competing interests of the carer and cared for centred around attempts to control the caregiving situation, and included whether and to what extent to involve services in their lives.

Although the health and well-being of the person and their carer are closely linked, the needs may not be the same and there may be times when their needs are in conflict (Williams and Robinson, 2001).

Lack of definitional clarity can offer some advantages due to the complexity of the shifting nature of dependency and caring roles through the life course. However, it can also present a challenge for individuals who find themselves in an intensive caring situation, who have not recognised themselves as carers, but are struggling to cope with the demands involved. When the relationships between two individuals changes due to accident or illness it can take time to acknowledge the impact of this (Cavaye, 2006), and coming to terms with the label 'carer' can involve a re-evaluation of one's own identity as well as the changed relationship with the cared-for person (Henderson, 2001). Definition can enable the individual to identify themselves as a carer and to seek support when required, and to encourage the health and social care system to identify and support the individual in a caring situation.

The term 'informal carer' was first used in the early 1980s to describe family members or friends who provided unpaid care, but the term did not enter a dictionary until the late 1980s (Cavaye, 2006). In the social care world in particular, many staff who provide direct support and care have been described as carers, especially since the 1990s (Cavaye, 2006). There is a need, therefore, to distinguish between people who are paid to provide care within structured employment, and those who find themselves in an unpaid caring role through personal circumstances. Two other terms used are unpaid carer and family carer, each with its own limitations. Some carers have identified that the title 'unpaid carer' makes their role seem of less value, while the title 'family carer' does not cover the role of unrelated individuals who might be playing significant caring roles. More recently, Fox *et al.* (2009), in their work on the carers' experience survey in England, found that the term 'expert carer' was often misunderstood. They settled for 'carer', which is the main term used in this book.

Policy context in relation to carers

The essential role carers play in supporting the majority of people with care and support needs to remain at home is now recognised in policy terms, although it is only recently that carers are explicitly cited. Cavaye (2006) traces the increasing emphasis on the role of carers to the New Right ideology associated with the Conservative government of the 1980s. She notes that, although the White Paper *Growing Older* did not specifically use the term 'carer,' it highlighted the primary sources of care for older people as informal: 'Care in the community must increasingly mean care by the community' (DHSS, 1981, p. 3). The term 'carer' emerged in policy by the end of the decade. The 1989 White Paper acknowledged that the bulk of community care is provided by friends, family and neighbours and 'that carers need help and support if they are to continue to carry out their role' (DH, 1989, p. 4).

Attention turned to carers' assessments in the 1990s, following the 1990 NHS and Community Care Act. It is sixteen years since the 1995 Carers (Recognition and Services) Act entitled carers who regularly provide substantial amounts of care to request an assessment of their needs. The carer's right to an assessment was triggered when the cared-for person was assessed. Although the 1995 Act was a significant achievement for carers' organisations, there is little indication that the legislation made much difference to the level of services provided for older people and their carers, which is unsurprising given that there were no extra resources to implement the requirements of the legislation (Cavaye, 2006).

In England, the right to an assessment was subsequently extended by the 2000 Carers and Disabled Children's Act, which applies to carers over the age of sixteen. The 2000 Act underscored the importance of developing services for carers that reflect carer-defined outcomes and support carers in their role. Since then, the carer's right to an assessment is no longer tied to the assessment of the cared-for person. However, evidence subsequent to the 2000 Act indicated both that carers remained unsure about their right to an assessment (Seddon and Robinson, 2001; Carers UK, 2003) and that carers' assessments were not widely promoted (Audit Commission, 2004). The 2004 Carers (Equal Opportunities) Act subsequently placed a duty on local authorities to inform carers about their rights.

In parallel to this in Scotland, the Community Care and Health (Scotland) Act 2002 made provision for the right to a carer assessment independent of the cared-for person. Local authorities were required to recognise the views of a carer in deciding what services to offer to the cared-for person. NHS Boards were required to draw up carers' information strategies informing carers of their rights under this legislation. The National Minimum Standards for assessment, care planning and review (Scottish Government, 2008) included a particular focus on outcomes in the standards for carers' assessment. However, take-up of carers' assessment remains low in Scotland, England and Wales.

More recently in Scotland, *Caring Together: The Carers Strategy* (Scottish Government, 2010b) recognises carers as partners in the delivery of care and sets out ten key actions to improve support to carers with a focus on improved identification of carers, assessment, information and advice, health and well-being, carer support, participation and partnership. This strategy sits alongside the policy programme *Reshaping Care for Older People* (Scottish Government, 2011), with its emphasis on shifting resources to care at home. The *Carers Strategy* maintains that activity should focus on identifying, assessing and supporting carers in a personalised and outcomes-focused way. It acknowledges continuing difficulties of collecting data on black and minority ethnic carers and that not enough is known about carers with disabilities, gypsy travellers and refugees, which should be addressed. It identifies a need to build innovative approaches to short breaks, including in rural populations. It also identifies the intention to develop a Carers' Rights Charter to consolidate carers' rights.

Outcomes for and partnership with unpaid carers

As discussed in Chapter 1, when work on outcomes began with the Joint Improvement Team, it was identified that a separate strand of work was required on pinpointing outcomes for carers. This work was quickly taken forward following initial consultancy with partnerships, with the additional objective of working with stakeholders on developing associated tools (Miller, 2007). In parallel to the preceding MASC project with service users, this project began with a review of previous work done by SPRU on carers, which had identified four broad categories of carer outcomes, as set out in the headings in Table 3.1. Joint work was then undertaken between Voice of Carers Across Lothian (VOCAL) and the JIT in running focus groups with carers to test the salience of the SPRU outcomes.

The work by SPRU had included a number of outcomes relating to the quality of life of the cared-for person. However, during the carers' focus groups, it proved challenging to encourage carers to move away from talking about their concerns about the cared-for person in order to focus on their own quality of life. It was agreed that it might be preferable to concentrate the focus on the cared-for person, around one general outcome. Overall, the outcomes identified by SPRU were found to relate well to carers' experiences and few modifications were made overall. The key quality-of-life outcomes for people are basically the same as those identified by SPRU.

Table 3.1: Outcomes important to carers.

Quality of life for the cared-for person	Quality of life for the carer	Managing the caring role	Process
Ensuring quality of life for the cared-for person is achieved	Maintaining health and well-being	Choices in caring, including the limits of caring	Valued/respected and expertise recognised
	A life of their own	Feeling informed/skilled/equipped	Having a say in services
	Positive relationship with person cared for	Satisfaction in caring	Flexible and responsive to changing needs
	Freedom from financial hardship	Partnership with services	Positive/meaningful relationship with practitioners
			Accessible, available and free at the point of need

When this work was undertaken, the developing outcomes approach was still known as UDSET. A different term was required for a framework of carers' outcomes, and the term adopted at the time was the Carer Defined Service Evaluation Toolkit (CDSET), before the new overall term Talking Points was introduced. Following the initial focus group work, subsequent testing out and development of tools were undertaken with practitioners and carers in early implementer sites in Orkney and East Renfrewshire. Two different approaches were taken in these sites. In Orkney, the carers' centre, which was already charged with undertaking carers' assessments, was assigned the role of piloting the outcomes-focused review. The small staff team involved responded positively to the outcomes approach, which they saw as building on their existing work, while enabling them to evidence its benefits. In East Renfrewshire, a different approach was adopted, with health and social work staff undergoing training in outcomes and carers' assessment. As with previous research on outcomes (Guberman *et al.,* 2003), this work demonstrated that exchanges based on outcomes provided opportunities to improve communication with users and carers and supported improved decision-making and more relevant interventions, with some key comments as below:

- It gives you the opportunity to look at your situation from a different viewpoint; (Carer, East Renfrewshire)
- Most of the care plans resulting from our carer assessments involved modest inputs: access to information, peer support or one-off sessions with professionals; (Team leader, East Renfrewshire)
- Moving from an NHS type of assessment to holistic assessment was daunting to start with and involved a different way of thinking but I now prefer this approach (Physiotherapist, East Renfrewshire). (Cook *et al.,* 2007)

This piloting work coincided with an opportunity to work alongside a lottery-funded project on digital stories in health and social care. The digital stories were to have a significant impact on the knowledge-exchange aspect of the programme. Digital stories, lasting just a few minutes long, combined an individual's personal story, recorded in audio, with still images and music. These stories have proven to be an essential tool in conveying the potential of an outcomes approach at events and staff development sessions. Several digital stories were made from the two carers' outcomes pilot sites, involving both carers and staff. These digital stories were found to be particularly powerful and one carer's story in particular, *Christeen's story*, was subsequently shown at a range of local and national events. This story highlighted a range of themes, but perhaps the strongest theme to emerge related back to the importance of skilled communication. Christeen, who is quoted at the opening of this chapter, identified how the conversation with the professional for the assessment had enabled her 'to think about her life from a different viewpoint', to recognise that she had locked herself into a role that was affecting her health, and that she needed to let others, including her family and services, support her more. The psychosocial benefits of a carer's assessment has recently been further evidenced by research in Wales (Stock and Lambert, 2011), including the importance to carers of being listened to, to have their role validated and valued and to consider hopes and fears for the future.

Continued challenges and possibilities in improving outcomes for carers

The early work on developing assessment and review with carers gave rise to some optimism. Carers identified positive impacts from outcomes-focused assessment and reviews. Practitioners who had been sceptical about carers' assessment described positive outcomes both for the carers and themselves. The National Carers Organisations (NCOs) in Scotland responded enthusiastically to the outcomes agenda and collaborated with the Assessment Review Co-ordinating Group (ARCG) on producing the national minimum information standards for carers' assessment, support planning and review. However, in the early implementation work, what emerged repeatedly were the limitations of engagement between statutory agencies and unpaid carers. Some staff confirmed that they, justifiably, focus primarily on the service user in the work they do. However, many staff acknowledged that, given time constraints, this can take place to the exclusion of the carer. Staff also expressed reservations about undertaking carers' assessments/support plans because of concern about 'raising expectations' of carers in a resource-limited service world.

A challenge still remains to convince both practitioners and carers of the positive outcomes that can arise from a carer assessment when conducted in a timely and sensitive manner. Practitioners need to engage positively with carers about their right to an assessment, make its purpose and process explicit and minimise anxieties surrounding the process. There is no doubt that there are carers who are desperate for a break from their caring role and new more sustainable ways will have to be found of ensuring that carers who need this are supported in a variety of ways, as identified in Scottish research on Short Breaks (Reid Howie, 2010). Meanwhile, work with carers continues to confirm that while access to quality services is important to some, what most carers want is acknowledgement of their caring role, to be listened to and to gain access to other sources of support (Gillies, 2000). The central concern of carers to be treated as partners is, however, hindered by staff concerns about their role as gatekeepers (Miller *et al.*, 2008; Jarvis, 2010). This situation is echoed by research in Wales, which identifies missed opportunities in improving outcomes for carers, and that, 'contrary to staff perceptions, carers reported modest requests for assistance' (Seddon *et al.*, 2006, p. 1483). More recent research in Wales has highlighted carers' needs as a 'wicked issue', which requires innovation and creativity: 'thinking around carers' problems needs to be holistic and not cemented in old, linear patterns' (Stock and Lambert, 2011, p. 181).

There are continuing challenges about making carers' assessments manageable and meaningful. Seddon's research found that most carer assessment protocols were narrow in focus and overly task-oriented, taking insufficient account of psychosocial and relational aspects of caring:

> Carers feel constrained by highly structured 'tick-box' assessment protocols administered by some practitioners or left for self-completion. Staff report low return rates and give very limited feedback to carers who complete this type of assessment. Whilst a carer assessment protocol may be made available to carers to help them prepare for a carer assessment, most carers and practitioners agree that it is a poor substitute for face-to-face contact (Seddon *et al.*, 2006, p. 1345).

Limited recognition of carers' emotional needs is of particular concern. Carers experiencing high levels of stress are most likely to experience ill health, and in turn become users of health and social care services in their own right (Hirst, 2005). Many unpaid carers suffer from both stress-related illnesses and physical health problems with an increased risk of poverty (Carers UK, 2008). On the whole, there have been areas of progress. Pressure groups, which emerged from the early 80s, have had a key role in raising the profile of carers (Cavaye, 2006). The voluntary sector has burgeoned in relation to carers' support and advocacy in the past twenty years, and in many areas responsibility for supporting carers is largely devolved to the voluntary sector. However, where statutory services continue to fail to engage with carers, this has critical implications for relationships between carers and services, and for carers' ability to continue coping with caring. Avoiding carers' outcomes now leads to increased demand later.

In developing outcomes-based working in Scotland, there has been greater progress with regard to service users than with carers in the first few years. However, it is clear early in 2011 that some local areas are working actively to improve carer engagement around outcomes. Some additional impetus has emerged from the *Reshaping Care for Older People* programme (Scottish Government, 2011), with its focus on demographic pressures and the need to develop more sustainable ways of working. The associated Change Fund allocations early in 2011 made to all partnership areas included a requirement to develop their local carer support activity. It will be interesting to monitor how much of the intended innovation work materialises with regard to work with carers.

Conclusion

Beginning with early assumptions about the role of housewives in providing care for all dependents at home, the welfare state has traditionally shown reluctance to fund domiciliary support for fear of undermining continued family care. This perception that provision of support would undermine the willingness of families to carry out their obligations was challenged by research by Townsend (1968), who found the support services were, in fact, essential to enable many to continue caring, and subsequently by Moroney (1976), who argued that lack of support was likely to lead to many more breakdowns of caring relationships. Cavaye's (2006) work on hidden carers shows that, in fact, many carers strive as hard as they can to care independently for as long as they can manage, highlighting the importance of support being available when carers are struggling to continue. Recently, there has been increasing policy acknowledgement of the needs and outcomes of carers.

Unlike the other chapters in this book, it is less evident that the 1990 Act had a significant impact on carers, in the ways that other players in the system were affected by the legislation. This is largely because much of the policy on carers' assessment followed the 1990 Health and Social Care Act, so that it is not possible in the same way to compare before and after. However, the literature does suggest that the fact that carers' assessment was introduced alongside increasing pressure on care managers to ration resources has influenced the low level of uptake. It is clear from the UK literature and the experience of introducing outcomes-based working in Scotland that the concern of care managers to avoid raising expectations is a continuing barrier.

Whilst acknowledging the valid range of concerns about separating service users' from carers' issues, this book has included a separate chapter on carers because it is a book about outcomes, and carer outcomes are to an extent distinct, because of the ambiguous position they occupy in the health and social care system. Carers are not always accepted as legitimate recipients of support and services in their own right, nor are they routinely included as partners by services. Recent policy includes an increasing focus on outcomes, and outcomes-based working does offer some potential to progress from the tensions inherent in needs-led assessment, the challenges of the economic downturn notwithstanding.

Much of the work underway in local areas early in 2011 is centred on developing more streamlined approaches to carers' assessment/support plans, including an increased focus on outcomes. Carers' assessments provide one means of identifying and supporting carers, and as evidenced in Christeen's story a skilled exchange between a member of staff and a carer can itself improve outcomes for the carer. Additional benefits from carers' assessment and review are the potential to improve the evidence base, because much of the support that is already provided to carers in local areas is not recorded. In a wider sense, the potential to improve understanding of the interactions between supports, services and outcomes is significant.

CHAPTER 4

Better Outcomes for Staff

> I had worked abroad for ten years and then decided to come
> back to Scotland about two years ago. I couldn't believe how
> much the whole terrain had shifted in the time I was away
> ... This wasn't social work anymore as I understood it. It
> wasn't about working with people in the same way, and I
> understood for the first time that I need to relate to the
> people I work with as much as they need me. That's why this
> outcomes work is important to me, it's about those values,
> about building relationships with people (Care manager,
> Talking Points early implementer area).

This chapter will consider the position of frontline staff in health
and social care in the community, including staff perspectives on
outcomes-based working. This discussion will involve development
of themes raised in the first chapter, including staff being caught
between a variety of competing imperatives which sometimes conflict with their values. As with previous chapters, this will include
emphasis on the impact of the 1990 Health and Community Care
Act. Chapter 4 is based on the premise that better outcomes for staff
are a prerequisite if the outcomes agenda is to result in improvements
to service users and carers. Most of the literature on the impact of
care management on staff centres on social work and social care
staff, with less attention to nurses, who became involved as care
managers at a later stage and to a lesser extent. However, issues of
relevance to both NHS and local authority staff will be considered
here in relation to how a personal-outcomes approach can be integrated into practice.

Staff relationships with service users and carers, and power

There is a significant literature highlighting the importance of relationships and emotions in health and social care services, both in relation to improved well-being of people using services (Morrison, 2007; Bell and Smerdon, 2011) and improved resilience and commitment amongst staff (Yoo, 2002). Morrison (2007) argues that organisations need to broaden the focus for staff development beyond achievement of competence. Morrison refers to work by Benner (1984), who conducted research on competence in nursing practice in the USA. Benner's analysis of critical-incident interviews with experienced nurses identifies that the expert nurse had levels of anticipatory, observational, analytical and inter-personal patient care skills that were frequently life-saving. This was achieved both by intervening speedily during medical crises, and by making powerful emotional contact with the patient that motivated their self-healing determination. Concerns about the shift towards overly technical approaches to care are evident in both health and social care. In his work on emotional intelligence, Benner (1984) highlights the risks of a purely technical set of competences, in which such expertise is neither described nor valued. Webb (2006) highlights how economic and technical rationality have been combined to calculate probabilities of risk, transforming practitioners into administrative executants, administering technologies of care.

As discussed in Chapter 1, managerialism emerged from monetarist policies, which took hold in the UK during the 1980s. Public choice protagonists at this time argued against the notion of public servants and politicians working for 'the public interest', based on the assumption that the notion of altruism was false. From this perspective, professionals were presented as motivated by self-interest, exercising power over 'would-be customers' and blocking choice through their claim to professional knowledge (Clarke and Newman, 1997). The only true democracy was a free market in which consumers could act on their desires in accessing services, making choices and influencing service provision:

> While choice is thought of as the external driver for improvement, the complementary internal mechanisms are targets

and incentives which, in the model, drive public servants to work in their own self-interest. The ends are determined by the policymakers, the means are determined by those who have been incentivised to meet their targets. (Seddon, 2008, p. 7)

Writing before the implementation of care management, Lipsky (1980) introduced the theory of street-level bureaucracy, asserting the power of staff as policy implementers and their consequent influence on public policies. From this perspective, professionals are situated at the interface between policy and the public, where they face an ongoing duality between being responsive to their clients' needs and ensuring policies are properly implemented. The professional training they receive before qualifying teaches them about the principles of practice, but less about the role conflicts that exist at the interface. The dilemmas posed to these actors force them to adopt reactionary strategies in order to cope with the challenges of the job — strategies that range from rationing resources to screening and routinising clients. Lipsky (1980) argues that street-level bureaucrats have intimate knowledge of resources and a clearer understanding of their clients. Those resources, coupled with strong discretionary capacity and interpretative ability, form the basis for stark influence on the intent of policies. More recently, Evans and Harris (2004) argue that more rules may create more discretion, and that the exercise of professional discretion by street-level bureaucrats is not inherently 'bad', but can be seen as an important professional attribute. However, as will be discussed in the following section, much of the literature on care management following the 1990 Act suggests that the degree of discretion can be marginal, representing a dilute form of power.

Specific impacts of care management

A key consideration in this chapter is the influence of care management on frontline practice, with a focus on the implications for relationships and professional practice. Much of the literature on this topic is weighted towards the social work profession, with some references to health. The account given here does not start from the assumption that there was a 'golden age' of user and carer involvement prior to care management. Postle (2001) cautions against a simplistic contrast between unfavourable references to care management as compared to a social work ideal, which she argues 'runs the risk of ignoring the lack of clarity and the inherent ambiguity of the social work role'.

As suggested in the opening to this chapter, community care reforms from 1990 continued and in some senses accentuated existing tensions in health and social care, particularly as emphasis was placed on the creation of 'needs-led' services within continuing limitations on public expenditure. Rummery (2002) commented on the tendency of local authorities to focus on administrative aspects of care management — perhaps not a surprising response to organisational turbulence and financial stringency. Bureaucratic responses were adopted to manage scarcity of resources, with ever-tightening lines drawn around definitions of who is entitled to receive services. Two concepts, risk and dependency, are widely used to determine eligibility. While there were tensions and ambiguities around professional–public relationships prior to the 1990 Act, the view that care management shifted the balance so that bureaucracy overshadowed direct work with service users is widespread and supported by a significant body of research (Hugman, 1994; Henwood, 2001; Postle, 2002; Means *et al.*, 2008). Postle (2002) found a significant decrease in job satisfaction and high levels of stress-related illness amongst social workers working with older people, which seemed to be linked to difficulties reconciling different aspects of their role.

Relevant policy guidance (DH/SSI, 1991) identified that the needs of the service user were to be identified through the assessment process. While the user was to express their preferences through this process, the practitioner would identify the needs (Means *et al.*, 2008). These authors also identify that the communication skills required for good assessment were restricted through care management:

> Good assessment ... requires highly developed communications and interpersonal skills and a capacity for reflective practice. However, evidence from research suggests that, although good practice exists, the way in which assessment and care management systems have been implemented may have restricted the use and development of such skills. (Means *et al.*, 2008, p. 62)

While the guidance acknowledges that the relationship between the user and the professional will 'never be totally equal', practitioners were advised to correct the imbalance by sharing information and involving individuals as far as possible in decision-making (DH/SSI, 1991, p. 16). However, in reality, the power to define what counts as 'need' would rest not with the practitioner but with the local authority, whose role is to provide services to individuals whose needs fall within published eligibility criteria (Means *et al.*, 2008).

In their account of professional motivation, Martin *et al.* (2004) identify how professionals were recast in policy terms from their role as publicly interested 'knights' to self-interested 'knaves'. Rather than assuming that self-interest is the natural order, however, these authors argue for consideration of organisational context in shaping human behaviours. In their research on practitioner responses to care management, they found that bureaucracy and budgeting shaped practitioner behaviour, but they also point out notable exceptions which involved providers and care managers going beyond their prescribed roles, sometimes at risk to their own jobs, to meet needs that they felt were required for that individual. While these authors acknowledge that it is too challenging to be able to make evidence-based claims about the intrinsic motivations of professionals they argue that policy predicated on the notion of practitioners as self-interested knaves actually creates the kinds of behaviour that it wishes to negate. Meanwhile, continuing the analogy started earlier by Le Grand (1997), staff can be recast neither as knights or knaves, but as 'pawns whose responsibility it is to ensure that the will of the department is carried out' (Martin *et al.*, 2004, p. 482). More recent research by Sullivan (2009) investigated the impacts of care management on professional practice, finding that practitioners often adopt frames of reference which allow them to interpret events and sometimes service users in ways that fit with the requirements of the system, in order to manage the tensions and contradictions within their role. This could result in service users being caught in 'frame traps' (Goffman, 1974), which meant that they were not listened to, and sometimes actively blocked from introducing their own frames into the encounter.

The reality is that, just as service users and carers respond differently and adopt a range of strategies in response to challenges and difficulties in their lives, practitioners manage role ambiguities in different ways. Frontline practitioners have been shown to create their own barriers to provision to manage an overwhelming workload (e.g. Lipsky, 1980; Rummery and Glendinning, 1999; Sullivan, 2009). Postle (2002) studied care managers working with older people, identifying five positions of tension in the care management role (see Table 4.1).

Table 4.1: Tensions and ambiguities in the care management role (Postle, 2002).

Emphasis on assessment of needs	Restricted resources to meet needs
Working with the person	Focusing on the minutiae of financial assessments
Taking time to develop a relationship	Spending time on paperwork and IT
Increasingly complex work	More reductionist processes such as checklists
Concern about all aspects of risk	Speed of work through-put increasing risk

Work undertaken by the Audit Commission on staff motivations for working in the public sector, as well as reasons for leaving, was reported in 2002. Amongst a variety of motivational factors, making a difference to other people was the single biggest factor attracting people. The factors that caused people to leave were predominantly those associated with managerialism, with bureaucracy and paperwork being the most commonly cited, as well as lack of resources and too many targets:

> Many felt that the content of their work was increasingly driven not by what matters but by what could be measured ... Targets are important to demonstrate the link between what individuals do and what organisations do, but they need to be few and their relevance evident. Our study suggests that too many public sector staff do not see how performance measurement relates to their own primary goal to make a positive difference in people's lives. (Audit Commission, 2002, p. 23)

Some 55% of respondents in the survey said that the number of change initiatives had had a significant impact on their decision to leave. Not being valued by various stakeholders was cited as an important factor in workers' decisions to leave, and this supports the case for improving outcomes for staff. The negative impact of the pace of change was seen in the focus groups as a specifically public sector problem, with new initiatives viewed neither as listening to or involving staff but as top-down government initiatives.

With regard to health and social care specifically, more than a decade after the 1990 Act it was evident that community care assessment had failed to deliver on initial goals. This resulted in a shift in emphasis from 2000, with attention moving to developing community care assessment, which would be shared across health and social care services, and to greater emphasis on involving nursing staff as care managers.

Shared assessment in health and social care in the community

The introduction of care management was viewed in policy terms as offering opportunities to improve partnership working between health and social care, as well as between staff and service users. Social services were initially given the lead role in conducting assessments of the needs of individuals, in collaboration with other professionals. However, the different funding arrangements for health and social care services meant that service users and carers could still be subject to both assessment and care management and the nursing process (McNally *et al.*, 2003).

A more recent literature review on shared assessment in the UK (Miller and Cameron, 2011) confirms that the introduction of shared assessment brought with it a further cascade of change for health and social care, including requirements to develop new tools and information-sharing protocols and processes, to find ways of sharing information between IT systems and to provide training to a range of professional staff in assessment and care management.

Although it is clearly undesirable for an individual to have to tell their story repeatedly as they interact with various professionals at different points in their pathway through services, the literature review confirmed that assessment became more arduous, both for professionals and the person being assessed. The information requirements were onerous, in the endeavour to ensure that both agencies' requirements and a range of performance data were gathered. Frustration was compounded by the fact that electronic solutions to data sharing did not materialise in most areas. A further issue for staff was the sense that assessment, symbolic of the impacts of managerialism on wider practice, became increasingly prescribed. In particular, standardisation of assessment impeded the flexible communication known to be required to ensure that all individuals being assessed are able to be fully included in decision-making (Miller and Cameron, 2011). Additionally, the requirement for staff to balance user-defined need against fixed-agency eligibility criteria in framing decisions about support and services was highlighted as representing an issue of real conflict for practitioners (Abendstern *et al.*, 2008). The requirement for staff to focus on needs as a means of establishing eligibility mean that staff are encouraged to focus on what the person or carer is unable to do, to focus on their problems and deficits and commensurate risks, in order to establish a sufficiently high band to be able to access services. The lack of attention to outcomes, goal-setting and involvement of the person in assessment is inconsistent with person-centred, personalised and preventive services.

Recent policies in Scotland have sought to renew the emphasis on person-centred practice in health and social care. Social work was subject to a review process resulting in the publication of *Changing Lives* (Scottish Government, 2006). The review acknowledged the constraints on social work practice through gatekeeping and bureaucracy and emphasised the need to empower frontline staff in order that they could in turn adopt more person-centred practice, which worked to maximise the strengths of each individual. The more recent NHS *Quality Strategy* in Scotland (Scottish Government, 2010a) sets out the intention to realise the three quality ambitions: person-centred, safe and effective. The emphasis is on developing a quality-measurement framework to set out measures and targets to monitor, challenge, support and report progress. The aims are to improve and embed patient-reported outcomes, support partnership between staff, patients and carers and support self-management by patients. Feedback during the consultation phase of the Quality Strategy included a request from the Royal College of Nursing (RCN) in Scotland for a radical rethink of the performance-management regime:

Currently staff experience an NHS culture which is dominated by the imperative to deliver on targets. In some areas this is a long way from a culture which enhances a relationship-based approach to improving the patient report outcomes and experience. (Fyffe, 2009, p. 3)

Again, reflecting the need to improve outcomes for staff, the need to more actively engage staff in defining the terms, and as partners in the culture shift, was also identified.

Outcomes-based working as a potential way forward

Outcomes-focused work is founded on the concept of a conversation, based around the outcomes that research shows are important to people. Practitioners are, therefore, establishing rapport and listening to the person's 'story'. Where practitioners have become used to predetermined question-and-answer formats, it can be a challenge to move towards less structured formats. There is significant skill involved in being able to work flexibly around a framework of outcomes, allowing the person to determine the order in which they want to talk about their lives, based on their knowledge of their situation, while ensuring that core areas are covered. Although devised around twenty years ago, the model developed by Smale *et al.* (1993) remains relevant to current practice. Smale *et al.* describe three models of assessment:

- *the questioning model* — where the *assessor* is the expert and asks all the questions in order to determine what the person needs;
- *the procedural model* — where the *forms and procedures* are the expert and the assessor just follows instructions which will determine what services should be provided;
- *the exchange model* — where *everyone* is an expert, including the assessor, service user (by experience) and carer; assessments and planning including review are therefore co-produced.

The managerial approach to assessment and care management has tended towards a combination of the questioning and the procedural model. An outcomes approach would support the exchange model, where the strengths, capacity and aspirations of the services users are central to the assessment. This model has been found to resonate with practitioners implementing outcomes-based working.

In this section, further consideration will be given to early evidence from England and emerging evidence from Scotland and Wales on the potential benefits of outcomes-based approaches to assessment. Much of this section has also been published as a journal article (Miller, 2010). To take the early work from England first, one of the key challenges identified is the investment required to support the change in culture. Although some staff may easily adopt an outcomes perspective, for many others opportunities for training, discussion and practice are important facilitators in achieving the culture change required (Qureshi and Nicholas, 2001). With regard to benefits, early research by SPRU undertaken with older people suggests that, once professionals have a clear understanding of the concept of outcomes, then the identification of agreed intended outcomes during assessment helps to focus intervention on the desired aims of services and the aims and preferences of users. It also provides a clear basis for planning and briefing providers (Qureshi, 2001). Slightly later work by SPRU confirmed a number of specific benefits from this approach which contributed to person-centred practice:

- assessment process more focused;
- gave attention to aspirations and not just problems;
- highlighted the user's and carer's sense of priorities;
- greater recognition for carers;
- made care plans more creative;
- clearer guidance for providers about the purpose of help and individual preferences;
- clarified differences in perspectives, which could assist negotiation;
- feedback about the impact of services helped in fine-tuning care packages. (Ball et al., 2004, p. 15)

There have been continuing examples of outcomes-based innovations in England in more recent years. One example is work undertaken in Thurrock Council. An inspection report from the Commission for Social Care Inspection (CSCI, 2008) highlights a range of positive findings including:

- a determined and increasing focus on outcomes for people through the adoption of an 'outcomes-based commissioning' approach;

- home care providers were increasingly flexible;
- the vision and values for adult social care were clear and becoming increasingly embedded across all partnerships. The senior management team were determined, driven and enthusiastic in their endeavour to transform adult services to promote independence, flexibility and choice;
- people were positive about the extent to which they were involved in decisions about their care and they felt that they were well supported;
- staff and key partners alike were signed up to the ambitious transformation plans;
- the Workforce Development Strategy was comprehensive and linked to local and national objectives.

In Wales, although outcomes-focused elements were incorporated into the Unified Assessment, a range of professional, technical and operational issues and requirements for further investment in staff development programmes were identified (Seddon *et al.*, 2010). Innovative work is underway in some areas, and outcomes-focused and relationship-centred pilots in Swansea produced positive early feedback from staff, providers and service users (Andrews *et al.*, 2009). In recognition of the importance of including better outcomes for staff, this work incorporated the 'Senses Framework', emphasising the inter-dependence between service users, carers and staff and the creation of 'enriched environments' of support (Nolan *et al.*, 2006). The aim is that service users, carers and frontline staff all achieve a sense of:

- security — to feel safe within relationships;
- belonging — to feel 'part of things';
- continuity — to experience links and consistency;
- purpose — to have a personally valuable goal or goals;
- achievement — to make progress towards a desired goal or goals;
- significance — to feel that 'you' matter.

In Scotland, the work on personal outcomes has been developed in partnership with the Joint Improvement Team, with its focus on supporting partnership working. Therefore, Talking Points has been promoted to both health and social care staff, in the statutory and third sectors, and more recently in the care-home and care-at-home sectors. In order to assess progress and barriers to implementing an outcomes approach, focus groups were undertaken with staff, frontline managers and senior managers in 2008 in one early implementer area where the focus at the time was social work staff. This exercise confirmed that a shift in the culture of social work in North Lanarkshire was evident. The focus on outcomes was viewed positively by staff at all levels for both restoring the values and principles of professional practice. The focus on outcomes was also viewed as providing a sense of clarity and purpose to practice and also as improving partnership working with service users. There was an additional concern in the managers' group to ensure that a methodology should be developed locally to measure and evidence outcomes, and to counterbalance existing performance indicators with user and carer outcomes. Otherwise, there was a risk that the outcomes approach would not endure (Miller and Johnstone, 2008).

Table 4.2 is based on learning from practice in Scotland and was produced to support understanding of the potential of the personal-outcomes approach to progress some of the policy priorities that have not been fully realised through previous service-led approaches to assessment in health and social care. The table highlights some of the lessons from outcomes-focused practice in Scotland, and the potential for outcomes to deliver on long-sought-after policy objectives in community care assessment, although not without caveats. Some of the emerging benefits from the outcomes approach were also amongst the expectations from needs-led assessment, following the 1990 Act, and subsequently from shared assessment. The review of shared assessment highlighted how competing priorities impeded realisation of the benefits of shared assessment, and there are continuing risks with the current focus on outcomes.

Although evidence from Scotland has shown that staff want to move from a perceived bureaucratic model to spend more time with people, it can still be a challenge to shift from a deficit or dependency approach to one that is not service-led (Jarvis, 2010), particularly where other elements in the system are still deficit focused. In considering some of the other elements, outcomes-based commissioning, performance management and eligibility criteria will be discussed from an organisational perspective in Chapter 5.

Table 4.2: Service-led and outcomes-focused approaches compared.

Service-led approaches	Outcomes-focused approaches
Tools encourage information gathering through standardised question-and-answer approaches to assessment, support planning and review	Semi-structured conversations with individuals in assessment, support planning and review
'Tick box' approach to assessment	Analytical skills involved in assessment
The person's views may be included in decision-making	The person's views/preferences are central to decision-making
The person is viewed as a client, service user or patient	The person is a citizen with rights and responsibilities
Where needs link to strict eligibility criteria, the assessor is required to maximise individual difficulties to access services	Involves consideration of difficulties, limitations and aspirations or goals. The priority is to identify what to work towards
If the person is deemed eligible, identified needs are matched to a limited range of block-provided services, resulting in service-driven approaches	Identifying outcomes involves considering a range of solutions/strategies including the role of the person, family supports and community-based resources
Where needs are tied to eligibility criteria, preventive work with people with low-level needs may be excluded	Outcomes allow preventive work to take place while services and resources are prioritised for those most in need
Focusing exclusively on deficits and difficulties, and how needs are to be met, results in a focus on tasks and in services that do things *to* people	By focusing on strengths, capacities and goals, while mindful of limitations, the role of the person is maximised. Services do things *with* people
Matching needs/deficits to services tends to result in static service delivery	Outcomes may change in the person's life journey and so should be revisited
Where outcomes are identified, these tend to be professional or organisational outcomes: e.g., improved nutrition or avoidance of delayed discharge	Outcomes are what matter to the person, though often consistent with professional and organisational outcomes: e.g., being able to get out and about
Starts from what services are currently available so restricts communication and limits options	Starts from the person's priorities so supports enabling relationships, creates clarity and identifies goals at an early stage. Being listened to, involved and respected supports better outcomes

Source: Miller *et al.*, 2009

Conclusion

The emphasis on form filling associated with care management has impacted on interactions between practitioners and users and carers. Although completing forms can help to develop a clear picture of the areas to be addressed, rigid adherence to predetermined criteria can distort communication and marginalise the individual: 'Time and energy could be wasted through exhaustive questioning that ultimately failed to capture the subtlety and complexity of individual needs' (Means *et al.*, 2008, p. 65). While there may still be a need for complex specialist assessments for some individuals, the starting point should be what matters to the person, and specialist assessments should link to the core outcomes for the individual.

Good communication is essential to build trust and rapport between individuals, and to develop relationships, which research shows are of fundamental importance to people using health and social care services, as well as to staff. A recent review of the literature (Bell and Smerdon, 2001) confirmed that the links between communication, relationships and outcomes are strongly supported by the evidence.

In addition to the trust and relationship building that is required to ensure that users and carers are genuinely involved in decision-making, acknowledgement of power differentials is essential (McPhail, 2008). However, while there are power differentials between staff and the public, the limitations of staff power also need to be acknowledged. Although staff have the advantage of being inside the system, with commensurate knowledge of how the system works, the literature shows that this knowledge does not necessarily translate into significant influence. Indeed, many of the outcomes identified as important by service users and carers also emerge in research about staff, with evidence that staff feel that they are not valued, listened to or treated with respect. Demoralised and disempowered staff cannot effectively support people who use services. A lack of honesty at various levels of the system about managing resource constraint, and a performance culture based on lack of trust, lead to high levels of tension at the front line. As discussed in Chapter 3, this is particularly evident in relation to work with carers, where conceptions about legitimacy become more blurred. While a more democratic relationship-based approach might not resolve issues about resource constraint, it does offer potential for progress. Outcomes-based working can support more open and relationship-based interactions, if a range of other system-based preconditions are met.

CHAPTER 5

Outcomes and Organisational Imperatives

> We've been working with our contracts and commission-
> ing staff and other key service designers to look at how we
> might be more flexible in the future ... If we start from a goal
> that someone wants to reach, we draw together much more
> cohesively the services, supports and resources that that
> individual and we have ... Because the other thing about
> the outcomes approach is that you do achieve goals. We just
> have to be more creative, we will find ways. But on that jour-
> ney we'll also discover 'What would be better if ...' Where
> did we not achieve and why not gives us the information
> we need to reshape our services. (Manager 'What Would
> be Better If' digital story on the JIT website)

Previous chapters have demonstrated the improvement potential
of an outcomes focus, in terms of supporting relationship building
between and better outcomes for staff, users and carers. However,
it is also clear that responsibility for outcomes-based working does
not just lie at the front line of services, but that there also needs
to be a wider re-orientation of systems at the organisational level.
Organisations are currently required to juggle a variety of competing imperatives, including those relating to eligibility, planning and
commissioning, performance, regulation and inspection, personalisation, marketisation and continuing restructuring to improve
partnership working, all with a diminished resource base. Although
some of these imperatives offer potential to achieve more efficient
use of existing resources, there are also inherent tensions between

them. Local areas are currently working out how to navigate between these tensions. This chapter will also involve consideration of key lessons from the change management literature, as well as the influence of wider policy.

Becoming an outcomes-focused organisation

One of the key messages from practitioners in developing outcomes-based working in Scotland has been the importance of 'high-level buy-in' to the outcomes agenda. This has been identified as necessary for three key reasons. The first is the requirement to re-orientate business processes and cultures to support new ways of working, which will be discussed in this section under the heading 'Organisational development'. The second is the need, frequently identified by practitioners, to have a clear signal that they have 'permission' to practise in less prescribed, more creative ways. This will be discussed under the heading 'Leadership for outcomes'. The third key reason is the need for a shift in how services are planned and commissioned, as well as consideration of which approach to performance management is adopted. These themes will be discussed under 'Key challenges to outcomes-based working'.

On a practical level, 'systems thinking' offers an alternative to the command-and-control management style, which Seddon (2008) describes. Consistent with managerialism, command and control has involved a preoccupation with the volume of work to be done, the number of staff, the time it takes staff to complete tasks and the associated costs. For Seddon (2008), the challenge is to move from a focus on costs to a focus on value, by ensuring that demands on the service that are caused by its own failures are rooted out. This includes investing time and resources on ensuring that the service gets it right at the outset: 'To take a systems view is to think about the organisation from the outside-in, to understand customer demand and to design a system that meets it' (Seddon, 2008, p. 71).

One of the advantages of a personal-outcomes approach is that it is not service-led, which means that the role of the person and other supports in their lives and communities are included as part of the picture, which supports more enabling relationships. With regard to the data generated from outcomes-based working, it is possible to

Table 5.1: It's a different way of thinking (Seddon, 2008, p. 70).

Command and control thinking		Systems thinking
Top-down hierarchy	**PERSPECTIVE**	Outside-in, system
Functional	**DESIGN**	Demand, flow and value
Separated from work	**DESIGN-MAKING**	Integrated with work
Output, targets, standards: related to budget	**MEASUREMENT**	Capability, variation: related to purpose
Contractual	**ATTITUDE TO CUSTOMERS**	What matters?
Contractual	**ATTITUDE TO SUPPLIERS**	Co-operative
Manage people and budgets	**ROLE OF MANAGEMENT**	Act on the system
Control	**ETHOS**	Learning
Reactive, projects	**CHANGE**	Adaptive, integral
Extrinsic	**MOTIVATION**	Intrinsic

include tick-box measures in support plans and review tools, which can produce easily quantifiable statistics about outcomes. However, analysis of a sample of qualitative data about outcomes can generate knowledge about what works. This can include understanding how individuals, either supported by the organisation or independently, have worked towards achieving their outcomes, as well as improved understanding of the barriers. As providers are currently facing increasing pressure to bid for diminishing contracts, there is commensurate pressure to demonstrate agency outcomes, which risks ignoring the individual's contribution. One of the concerns here is that where agencies implement user-satisfaction-type questionnaires, there is a probability of underestimating dissatisfaction (Cohen *et al.*, 1996; Hart, 1999) as compared to more qualitative conversation-based approaches, which engage with the complexity of people's lives (Cook and Miller, 2010).

With regard to implementing outcomes-based working, discussion of values within an organisation should include the extent to which the objectives are weighted towards improving outcomes and then being able to demonstrate better outcomes as a by-product, or whether the primary objective is proving how good the organisation is at delivering outcomes. Experience from the Talking Points programme has shown how tension emerges around outcomes-based innovations where the performance agenda is the driving force (Hitchins, 2010).

Organisational development

In general terms, there are many different ways of thinking about organisational change. A previous literature review by Iles and Sutherland (2001) highlighted the diversity of concepts and processes involved:

- developmental — improving current situation;
- transitional — implementation of a known desired state (episodic);
- transformational — new state gradually emerges, unknown until it takes shape.

In their work on outcomes, SPRU identified that implementing outcomes-focused practice and information systems was most likely to be developmental and continuous, involving adaptation of ideas to suit circumstances, experimentation on a small scale, leading to incremental learning. They also argue that, with planned and sustained effort, these incremental initiatives could have a 'transformational' impact in time (Nicholas *et al.*, 2003).

Figure 5.1: Understanding innovation in relation to outcomes-based working.

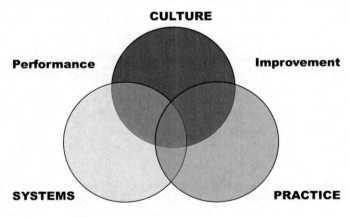

Smale (1996) stresses the importance of separating out the various innovations and identifying who is likely to be involved with each. Using this model, staff at SPRU identified that outcome-related innovation can include:

- culture change: a focus on impacts rather than inputs and outputs, greater recognition of different types of expertise (including user and carer);
- different approaches to practice: how and when assessments, plans and reviews are undertaken, finding out how to engage with and record user and carer outcomes;
- new procedures/tasks in the system: develop new forms, review administrative and IT systems. (Nicholas *et al.*, 2003)

The two additional dimensions of performance and improvement were added to the model through the recent work undertaken in Scotland.

The innovation trinity is a model at the core of the Managing Change and Innovation Programme of the former National Institute of Social Work (Smale, 1996; Smale, 1998). There have been many significant additions to the change-management literature since the 1990s. However, as with Smale *et al.*'s (1993) exchange model of assessment, the innovation trinity has been found to resonate with managers and staff implementing outcomes-based working. The three dimensions of change reflect the complexity of the real world, serving to highlight overlapping areas of development activity.

Figure 5.2: The innovation trinity (Smale, 1998)

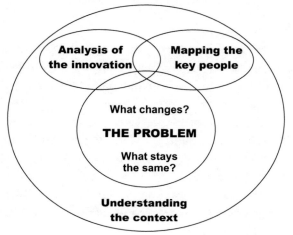

Mapping the significant people is the central dimension of the innovation trinity. This involves recognising the part played by key people in supporting or preventing change. Smale (1998) drew on previous work by Rogers (1995) in identifying the various roles, which include innovators, change agents, product champions, early adopters, late adopters, laggards, opinion leaders and gatekeepers, amongst others. These roles have proven relevant in implementing Talking Points, with the roles emerging within implementation sites as well as between different areas. The role of champions of the model, in particular, has been invaluable in so far as the champions are peers from within the organisation or from a neighbouring locality who can testify to the real world challenges and benefits of the approach.

Analysis of the innovation involves consideration of the nature of the planned change in relation to what processes might be employed and projected timescales. There are a range of project management tools which can support this type of analysis. Finally, understanding the context involves making use of compatible forces and avoiding potential conflicts. This would include consideration of the culture and relationships within the organisation, between key stakeholders and partner organisations and other areas of change. This is clearly of importance in considering work being implemented in partnership settings. There are also various project management tools to support this, including forcefield analysis (Lewin, 1951).

Leadership for outcomes

A further key message from implementing Talking Points has been that practitioners need ongoing support, particularly from frontline managers, to focus effectively on outcomes for people. Because of this, one of the objectives for the Talking Points programme was to produce outcomes-focused supervision guidance, which was developed with frontline line managers (Johnston and Miller, 2010). The importance of leadership in outcomes-based working was also prioritised by another organisation in Scotland from 2009 — the Institute for Research and Innovation in Social Services (IRISS), who produced a generic guide to leadership, followed up in 2011 by specific topic-based guides.

Signalling the lack of autonomy experienced by frontline staff under care management, the notion of permission has been raised repeatedly in the outcomes work, with a requirement for senior managers visibly to buy-in to the agenda. The idea of encouraging autonomy in staff is a theme in the supervision guidance, which highlights the need for outcomes-based working at all levels within the organisation. That is to say that, in parallel with the qualitative conversations taking place between staff and users and carers, similar conversations should take place between frontline managers and staff. This involves the manager listening carefully to what the staff member says about the situation they are working in, encouraging the worker to build on their own knowledge and strengths and to work towards solutions where possible (Johnston and Miller, 2010). The focus groups undertaken to inform the guidance highlighted that frontline managers in turn need support to be outcomes focused in the work that they do, and to know that it is safe for them to be more creative in the ways that they support their staff. In turn, senior management needs wider incentives to be aligned rather than contradicting with this approach, linking back to policy.

The concept of emotional intelligence has been identified by some early implementers as relevant to outcomes-based working. Chapter 4 included reference to the importance of emotional intelligence in staff relationships with service users. There is also a role for emotionally intelligent leadership. Emotional intelligence is not a new concept. For Goleman *et al.* (2002) positive emotionally intelligent leadership supports organisational goals by connecting these with individual goals, through democratic rather than hierarchical models of management, through valuing people's input and gaining commitment through participation There has been recent interest in emotional intelligence in social work (Morrison, 2007) and in the NHS (Akeriordet and Severinsson, 2008). It has been argued that improved emotional intelligence is essential to patient safety (Stanton and Noble, 2010) and to quality of healthcare and outcomes (Clarkson, 2009). Although emotional intelligence is a contested concept, particularly with regard to matters of measurability (Antonakis, 2009) and as to whether it is, in fact, a facet of personality rather than intelligence (Austin, 2008), the role of emotion in the organisation of human behaviour is well established (Morrison, 2007). The concept has also been found to resonate with staff and managers in implementing an outcomes approach.

Key challenges to outcomes-based working

This section will consider three key challenges that have been identified as presenting barriers to outcomes-based working: namely, eligibility criteria; performance management; and planning and commissioning. Staff and frontline managers have said that buy-in to outcomes-based working from senior management needs to extend beyond verbal support to a commitment to ensuring that business processes are redesigned to fit the new ways of working.

Eligibility

While there is clearly a need for consistency and fairness in decision-making about distribution of resources and services, the predominant existing approach has been found to be flawed. In particular, rigid imposition of Fair Access to Care Services (FACS) eligibility criteria presents a significant risk to outcomes-focused assessment and may result in further inefficiencies. The Institute of Public Care (2009) recently concluded that developing outcomes-based eligibility criteria need not necessarily call for a major overhaul of the eligibility system but rather its refinement and improved application. They identified three hurdles that require to be overcome:

- By tightly linking needs with resources, the eligibility process discourages other forms of help being brought into the package.
- Eligibility tests discourage a preventative approach because if people do not cross the threshold at the time of assessment they are not eligible for resources even though the acquisition of help now may prevent poor outcomes later.
- By making the eligibility threshold increasingly hard to cross, it encourages people to hold on to resources once obtained and hence provides no incentives for improvement either by the service user or the provider. (Institute of Public Care, 2009, p. 23)

In practice, some early implementers of the outcomes approach in Scotland have identified the eligibility criteria as a key challenge to progress, and work is underway in several areas to try to identify ways of implementing prioritisation in ways consistent with the outcomes focus.

Performance

Performance management is a particularly important theme for this book, because it has been identified that the improvement potential of a personal-outcomes approach can be undermined if the overarching focus becomes performance. The rationale for performance management includes improved accountability and transparency, learning and benchmarking and increasing output (de Bruijn, 2002). This reflects a shift in views about staff motivation and incentivisation associated with New Public Management, as identified in a recent review of the literature for the NHS Service Delivery and Organisation (SDO) programme: 'These initiatives reflect a general shift away from placing implicit trust in individuals and organisations to carry out their duties, towards actively managing their performance' (NHS: SDO, 2010, p. 1).

Performance management has traditionally focused on what can be measured, with a particular focus on outputs (de Bruijn, 2002). It also tends to start from system or strategic priorities rather than what matters to people using services, or staff. Indeed, concern has emerged that incentives to improve performance against national indicators might not improve outcomes for service users, as was found to be the case with hospital reimbursement for avoiding delayed discharges (CSCI, 2004; Clarkson, 2010), and that emergency admissions rose at the same time, adding weight to the view that incentives created by national reporting requirements divert energies from local monitoring and development of more integrated services (CSCI, 2004). Other concerns about unintended consequences of performance management include game-playing (de Bruijn, 2002; Bevan and Hood, 2006; Seddon, 2008) and blocking of innovation (de Bruijn, 2002). A much wider review of different accounts of the various pitfalls of performance management is available elsewhere (Van Thiel and Leeuw, 2002). As this range of concerns has emerged, considerable effort has been invested in developing countermeasures and systems to minimise the harmful effects of performance management (de Bruijn, 2002; Bevan and Hood, 2006):

> There is a systemic relationship between purpose, measures and method. In other words, this relationship is at work in any organisation, whether for good or bad. Imposing arbitrary measures in the shape of targets and standards creates a *de facto* purpose — meeting the targets — and constrains method, because the work gets designed round the reporting requirements. When measures are derived from purpose (from the customer's point of view), however, and when those measures are employed where the work is done, method is liberated. (Seddon, 2008, p. 82)

One of the key concerns associated with the performance management industry is the transfer of scarce organisational resources from service production and provision to information and monitoring systems (Hoggett, 1996; Clarke and Newman, 1997; de Bruijn, 2002). This is of particular concern in light of the economic downturn. Despite continuing problems of comparability and the identification of appropriate indicators, the intensity of competitiveness via rankings and league tables continues to raise concerns (Cutler and Waine, 1994; Seddon, 2008).

Recent research from the field of child protection in England highlights many similar concerns about the impact of managerialism on practice. Key messages centre on the failure of command-and-control approaches to improve management of risk (Laming, 2009; Munro, 2011). One study found that workers were pressurised to make early judgements, give creative accounts of their activity and take short cuts in order to maintain workflow (Broadhurst *et al.*, 2010). Other research found that the Integrated Children's System in England 'disrupted the professional task, engendering a range of unsafe practices and provoking a gathering storm of user resistance' (White *et al.*, 2010, p. 410). Contrary to the public-choice portrayal of the powerful professional, the research found that practitioners were not involved in the design of the system and that negative feedback from practice was ignored. This has recently resulted in recommendations that the views of practitioners need to be fed from the front line to all levels of management (Munro, 2011).

Some critics of the predominant performance management culture have made the case for alternative approaches, arguing that an exclusive focus on what's not working and why things go wrong undermines morale and learning and prevents forward movement (Barnes, 2004). Some have advocated more localised approaches that involve increased ownership by staff and contributions to organisational learning (Clarkson, 2010). Practitioners can use performance information generated by more participatory means, including through care planning where service user and carer outcomes can be recorded and analysed (Burnham, 2006). Another approach is Appreciative Inquiry (Barnes, 2004), which offers an opportunity to engage staff, stakeholders, service users and whole organisations in a process of positive improvement. Appreciative Inquiry was adopted by one of the implementers of Talking Points as a means of engaging the social work staff group in the change process (Upton, 2010). One of the key concerns arising from the implementation of Talking Points has been the need to develop confidence and skills in local organisations on qualitative analysis of outcomes data (Hitchins, 2010). Although some work was progressed on this aspect of the programme in the first two years, a decision was taken at the centre to discontinue support on qualitative data analysis until the quantitative measures in the Community Care Outcomes Framework were more firmly embedded. More recently, members of the Community Care Benchmarking Network have indicated significant interest in progressing use of qualitative data, and ensuring that user and carer outcomes are part of the performance picture.

Planning and commissioning
Sir Michael Lyons' (2007) review of the role, function and funding of local government identifies the vital role of local authorities in improving the well-being of a place and its inhabitants. Central to this view is the concept of place-shaping, which builds on existing structures such as planning processes and consultation. In other words, place-shaping involves studying demand and understanding what matters to people, and links that to strategy. Data derived from outcomes-based working can be an invaluable component of this.

Performance management targets interplay with how services are commissioned. If the primary drivers are to reduce admissions and reduce delayed discharges, there can be a tendency to invest significant resources in flagship services designed to improve performance on these targets. The MASC research highlighted in the opening chapter revealed a mixed picture of outcomes for older people according to which type of service was involved. Innovative services that had recently developed to relieve pressures on the acute sector, mainly intermediate care, involved well-resourced interdisciplinary teams who worked successfully to restore the confidence, skills and well-being of individuals. These services were, however, usually time limited (around six weeks). By contrast, people who had progressed to longer-term packages of home care, which were largely delivered on the basis of very short-time slots, reported poorer outcomes and a poor quality of care (Petch *et al.*, 2007). While investment in target-oriented services might achieve benefits in the short term, the lack of investment in longer-term support clearly sets up risks of a revolving door.

Chapter 2 included reference to how the intended aim of the 1990 Act to deliver integrated, responsive and efficient home care services proved more elusive than anticipated, largely due to a contracting culture based on task and time. More recently, attention has turned to developing care at home services with a focus on improving functional ability and quality of life (Ryburn *et al.*, 2009), resulting in reablement services within home care sectors in many localities. Current pressures on resources mean that services that offer potential to improve independence and potentially support people out of service use are attractive from a commissioning perspective. However, it is important that quality of life is considered as well as functional assessment, to avoid individuals experiencing decline following discharge from the service. A further note of caution is that, unless a more enabling culture is adopted in the wider sector, the outcomes of reablement might be short-lived, as people move between services. Reflecting back on the need to identify intended outcomes across services, in line with the concept of place-shaping, what is required is a 'root and branch change in the way in which mainstream services are commissioned and managed' (Slasberg, 2010, p. 149).

Rather than a target-driven approach, if the starting point is supporting people to live independently with the best quality of life possible, this leans towards a broader approach to commissioning, or place-shaping. A relatively recent development is a shift from over-rigid prescription of tasks in care at home, to allowing flexibility and responsiveness, through commissioning for outcomes (Sawyer, 2005). Time- as opposed to task-centred visits are easier to deliver punctually, with costs that are easier to calculate and that offer opportunities for flexibility or to just talk once essential jobs are finished (Glendinning *et al.*, 2006). A flexible approach allows the possibility of supportive relationships between users and care staff, and morale building (Patmore and McNulty, 2005) fitting with a preventive approach to depression among older people as proposed by Godfrey and Denby (2004). Alongside the shift in thinking about more flexible support to individuals, there has been a refocus on community development or Community Capacity Building as a means of supporting people to remain at home. Community Capacity Building is understood as: 'Activities, resources and support that strengthen the skills, abilities and confidence of people and community groups to take effective action and leading roles in the development of communities' (Home Office, 2003, p. 15) and has been identified as a key aspect of the *Reshaping Care for Older People* programme in Scotland (Scottish Government, 2011).

There is uncertainty at present about how commissioning and personalisation will interact. In England, there is a view that 'personalisation of public services is here to stay', with individual budgets the main delivery mechanism (Tizard, 2010, p. 44). Research has shown a range of concerns from commissioners around the need to recognise conflicts of interests and keep people safe in light of reduced staff involvement, about how to link concepts of total place or place-shaping with individual purchasing arrangements and the costs of running dual systems for an extended transition period (Needham, 2010). In Scotland, there is currently a strong emphasis on lead commissioning in adult health and social care, under which one or other body will be responsible for commissioning health and care services for designated groups (Samuel, 2011). At the same time, there is a drive to increase uptake of self-directed support in Scotland. The self-directed support strategy was launched at the end of 2010, with an ambition to make it 'the mainstream mechanism for the delivery of social care' (Dunning, 2010). The recent report from the Independent Commission on Social Services in Wales (2010) takes a broad view of commissioning, arguing for more joint commissioning and planning on the basis of the local community.

Engagement of the third sector in planning and commissioning of services has been identified as a gap across the UK. The missed potential to harness the expertise of the sector has been traced by Wyatt (2002) in England and the Coalition of Care and Support Providers north of the border (CCPS, 2002), while the recent Independent Commission on Social Care in Wales (2010) argues for more constructive engagement of the third sector in planning, designing and commissioning services. Outcomes-based commissioning requires a collaborative rather than adversarial approach between purchaser and provider agencies.

Conclusion

Outcomes-based working offers some potential for improved sustainability of public services in face of the economic downturn, because of its focus on strengths and capacities, maximising independence, and considering a wider range of resources than traditional services in order to achieve outcomes. However, there are various competing drivers in the system which need to be realigned if this potential is to be realised. Staff need to be freed up from unnecessary bureaucracy to be able to spend the upfront time with service users and carers, on which good decisions and enabling practice depend. Work in Wales has confirmed that increased emphasis on office-based data inputting has undermined practitioners' collective knowledge of community resources and consequent ability to support creative, cost-effective care planning (Andrews et al., 2009). Staff need space to get to know the alternative resources in the local communities in which they work, so they can link individuals back in and thus improve their quality of life, which can in itself constitute a form of community capacity building. With regard to service planning, the contention here is not that outcomes data should replace information about inputs and outputs, but rather that understanding what is working well and less well is currently the missing piece of the jigsaw with regard to place-shaping.

Whether you conceptualise staff motivation as intrinsic or extrinsic, organisations do shape behaviour and the importance of organisational values has been repeatedly highlighted in the literature (Audit Commission, 2002; Martin *et al.*, 2004). The starting point should be what matters to people, particularly users and carers but also staff, with a requirement to keep coming back to that point (Seddon, 2008). Amidst the range of current pressures, the challenge to put the person at the centre of systems is significant. Wider shifts required at an organisational level include a more outcomes-friendly system for determining eligibility, an approach to improvement which is less about arbitrary targets and more about meaningful measures and an outcomes-focused approach to planning and commissioning, along the lines of the place-shaping described by Lyons (2007).

CHAPTER 6

Getting Back to What Matters

> I fell into a trough [due to physical illness and bereavement] ... I went to the doctor who decided I might be slightly depressed ... The best thing that happened to me was first of all when Clare walked through the door ... You had somebody who you could ask silly questions of, who didn't get annoyed ... She listens to me and she's good to talk to because you can get all your thoughts in order ... It's the relationship with one person, that you talk about all your fears to, no matter how stupid. (Service user 'Building Relationships' digital story on the JIT website)

This chapter will review key themes from preceding chapters. While this account starts from overarching outcomes policy developments in Scotland, it then moves on to discuss issues of wider relevance, in considering the relationship between policy and organisational prerogatives and their influence on interactions at the front line. The main argument here is the need to align systems, processes and cultures to get back to what matters to the people who use health and social care services.

Strategic performance frameworks: The Single Outcome Agreement and the Community Care Outcomes Framework

A focus on personal outcomes has been evident in UK policy for some time. To recap on recent developments in Scotland, outcomes were given increased profile with the new concordat between national and local government when the SNP came to power (Scottish Government, 2007b). A continued commitment to outcomes was emphasised in a briefing from the Improvement Service (2011) prior to the re-election of the SNP government in spring 2011. While the concordat placed increased emphasis on the role of local government in driving local developments, the associated Single Outcome Agreement (SOA) required each local authority to make one report to central government on progress towards fifteen national outcomes, such as: 'We have improved the life chances for young children, young people and families at risk.' When doing this, the local authorities were to use the forty-five local indicators such as the one most relevant to health and social care: 'Increase the proportion of people needing care or support who are able to sustain an independent quality of life as part of the community, through effective joint working.'

As discussed in Chapter 1, the Community Care Outcomes Framework (CCOF) emerged in 2007 as the next iteration of the Joint Performance Information and Assessment Framework (JPIAF). JPIAF had focused on joint resourcing and management and Single Shared Assessment (SSA), or processes, rather than outcomes. The mix of sixteen measures in the CCOF includes four personal-outcomes measures amidst more traditional output and process measures. Further down at ground level, in the field of health and social care, outcomes-based working has been influenced by the approach known as Talking Points, a relative of the earlier SPRU approach to outcomes, which is also influential in England and Wales. This chapter will include a brief review of progress to early 2011, highlighting potential to get back to what matters to people, while acknowledging where tensions in the system continue to present barriers.

In principle, the SOA does offer some potential to reduce long-standing tensions in the balance of power between local and national government in Scotland. Scotland is a nation with significant geographical variation — ranging from urban through to very remote populations. A tendency to unequal power relations has been noted with reference to central policy imperatives that do not take account of local circumstances (McAteer and Bennett, 2005) or the significant challenges involved in policy implementation. The SOA, which is now the mandatory reporting framework, can be viewed as an initiative which seeks to achieve equity of outcomes, rather than uniformity of process. However, a change of culture is required at all levels of policy implementation for the benefits to be realised, with evidence that there is some way yet to go.

The SOA sets out high-level outcomes, based on an understanding that how they are to be achieved and monitored should be determined locally through Community Planning with NHS, housing and other partners. The philosophy, therefore, fits with the ground-level approach represented by Talking Points, whereby the outcome, or intended endpoint, is the starting point, leaving scope to determine how that outcome is best achieved. One of the challenges to developing a wider system that is genuinely outcomes focused is that achieving better outcomes requires a long-term view, which does not tend to fit with political cycles and pressures to demonstrate short-term gains. This challenge has been acknowledged by the Improvement Service (2011), who point out, for example, that ensuring that children's early years are happy and healthy makes it more likely that the rest of their lives will be the same, with benefits for communities and savings for public spending. The need to focus on longer-term outcomes was still not reflected across the system:

> Public service and business planning, budgeting, performance management and measurement, accountabilities, governance and scrutiny arrangements all remain more focused on the management of the services provided, rather than on the achievement of the outcomes we want from them. (Improvement Service, 2011, p. 4)

While the CCOF is not mandatory, the Community Care Benchmarking Network (CCBN), which took ownership of the framework from 2009, included at least one representative from each of the thirty-two partnership areas, in early 2011. In practice, sign-up to the measures in the framework varies significantly, with many local areas restricted to measures corresponding with NHS HEAT (health improvement, efficiency, access and treatment) targets, and a minority signed up to all or nearly all of the measures. A review of the CCOF began in 2010, involving interviews with stakeholders in local partnerships as well as in central government and national agencies. Although the personal-outcomes measures had not been prominent in the business agenda of the CCBN up until spring 2011, early findings from the review highlighted significant interest in raising their profile.

At ground level, a state of flux is continuing in community care early in 2011. During the past three-year period of intense activity on personal outcomes, a number of changes have been taking place, including: the introduction of mandatory eligibility criteria associated with concerns about equity of free personal and nursing care; an increased focus on self-directed support; a shift towards intermediate care and reablement in home care; implementation of telecare and telehealthcare; and an increased emphasis on self-management and co-production. These shifts are taking place amongst continuing emphasis on various aspects of partnership working. One of the challenges is that the culture of constant change does result in staff disengaging from initiatives (Eccles, 2008). While many of the initiatives have been incorporated in the *Reshaping Care for Older People* agenda (Scottish Government, 2011), tensions between some of the themes highlighted in earlier chapters in this book can present additional barriers to achieving buy-in from staff and managers.

There are opportunities amidst this state of flux to pull through lessons from previous periods of change, and to join up what might at first glance appear to be separate initiatives. One key lesson is the need to support the culture change involved, rather than fixating on process. When SSA was implemented in Scotland, the timetable set by central government was said to be unrealistically tight and implementation of central protocols at the local level described as uneven and difficult (Bruce and Forbes, 2005; McNamara, 2006; Eccles, 2008). Eccles (2008) notes that, although government circulars acknowledged the need for education, training and cultural engagement with staff, these aspects lagged behind: 'It is easy for those centrally involved in policy development to forget the layers of communication and information that have to be negotiated to reach frontline practitioners' (Petch, 2008, p. 79). In implementing the outcomes approach in Scotland, the practice side has not been formally supported, as compared to the performance management side. The performance agenda, represented by the CCOF, is supported by an active and comparatively well-resourced national network, the CCBN. The CCBN is progressing towards being funded by member subscriptions but has been centrally supported in the first two years. Limited attempts to address the gap in supporting practice included a session on personal outcomes at the quarterly benchmarking network in May 2011, where strong support was expressed for the need to improve links between practice and performance management. Lessons from the early days of developing and implementing Talking Points suggest that opportunities to share learning from practice would realise the additional benefits of avoiding each area having to struggle alone to develop systems and processes, and would also support greater consistency of understanding and implementation of policy.

Evaluating and managing performance at the centre

There are some signs that the performance culture in Scotland is evolving, with evident efforts at aligning performance and scrutiny demands post-Crerar review (2007), and with the increased emphasis on personal outcomes. However, there is some way to go before it could be said that the performance culture is either sustainable or measuring what matters. There is also a significant power imbalance with regard to who is subjected to routine evaluation. In particular, management of performance or systematic evaluation at policy level is not embedded. Another lesson which can be pulled through from the Joint Future Agenda concerns the need for evaluation of policy, in relation to both service impacts and service user and carer outcomes (Petch, 2008). With regard to policy performance more generally, three key themes emerge in recent literature as requiring attention: the need for policy coherence or joined-upness; improved acknowledgement of the organisational, resource and practice implications of policy implementation; and reduced policy hyperactivity. With regard to coherence, the tendency of sections of the Scottish Government to operate within silos has been noted elsewhere (Petch, 2008). In England, there is evidence that the increased focus on marketisation within health and social care serves to further complicate the picture:

> The policy landscape in England is complex, confusing and, at times, contradictory. A major complication is the absence

of a coherent national policy 'narrative', especially on the relationship between the twin imperatives of collaboration and competition. (Hudson, 2011)

Improved articulation of a value base including a coherent vision for public services is required. If public services, including the NHS and social services, are to flourish, Leys (2003) suggests that the public domain needs to be based on a clear philosophy, and a set of practical principles. With regard to policy hyperactivity and practice implications, it is recommended that the priority should shift to reducing implementation deficit and addressing the 'gap between rhetoric and reality on the ground' (Means *et al.*, 2008, p. 258). Questions which should be addressed before any new policy is implemented include:

- What is the overall vision for the policy area and how does the proposed policy fit with that?
- How does this policy fit with existing and emerging policies from other government sectors and the scrutiny bodies? Does this policy pass the joined-up test?
- Is this policy rooted in a well-established evidence base or does it still need to be trialled in practice to test for unintended consequences?
- What burden does this place on local systems and resources and is the burden justifiable in terms of anticipated benefits?
- Have other recent policy initiatives been given a chance to bed down before this one is issued?
- Are the organisational development implications sufficiently understood and are they being communicated effectively to those in practice?
- Who is responsible for monitoring the policy impact in practice and do local areas know who to contact with any issues?
- What systems have been put in place to allow sharing of good practice and emerging evidence about what is working well and less between local areas?

Consideration should also be given to evaluation of policy implementation, in ways that do not promote evaluation at the expense of improvement, and with a concern to monitor for unintended consequences. With regard to outcomes-based working in Scotland, there have been some efforts to capture evidence from the development and implementation of the personal-outcomes approach to date. However, this has been both opportunistic (including the capture of stakeholder perspectives at pre-existing meetings and events) and fragmentary (involving evaluations within local initiatives and pilots). An early stage national evaluation was undertaken by Glasgow School of Social Work (Stewart, 2008) but the agenda has progressed considerably since then. Current proposals are for a small-scale evaluation in 2011, which could at least capture a partial perspective on progress.

Interaction with practice

National policy undoubtedly influences structure, processes and cultures within local organisations. Experience of implementing outcomes-based working has also confirmed the extent to which local organisations are influenced by a range of other factors, including geography and demography. There is also significant variation in culture between different areas, as evident in the extent to which local organisations are driven by performance and/or improvement agendas, and related factors.

Returning to the theme of what motivates staff in public services, evidence shows that all of these factors in turn influence the behaviour of employees (Seddon, 2008). The majority of practitioners are motivated by the interests and improved well-being of the people they work with, sometimes finding ways of circumventing the rules in order to achieve these outcomes. However, research has repeatedly shown that managerialism has a negative impact on care managers' behaviour (Martin *et al.*, 2004), presenting significant barriers to staff being able to do a 'good job' based on principles of citizenship (Postle and Beresford, 2007).

From the perspective of staff, performance management tends to be viewed with suspicion. Doubts have frequently been expressed about whether outcomes are just 'another stick to beat us with' and whether outcomes-based working can be successfully implemented alongside existing performance indicators emphasising through-put. From a practitioner perspective, performance indicators and meeting government targets have become the focus of attention rather than the welfare of service users (Means *et al., 2008,* p. 209). If staff perceive that the system is placing barriers to them being able to do their job professionally and to make things better for the people they work for, they are going to be sceptical of any framework which they see as placing the blame for failures at their door. There have been examples in Scotland where outcomes information has been collated and discussed constructively with staff, including a focus on what is going well. This is in line with Seddon's (2008) assertion that the most important learning occurs at the front line, rather than a reliance on targets and bureaucratic performance systems built on relationships of mistrust.

In Scotland, the review of the CCOF could potentially result in a further step in the evolution of performance in community care in Scotland, if efforts to link with practice are realised. As shown in Chapter 5, performance management has attracted a significant critical body of evidence about gaming the system, unintended and sometimes harmful consequences whilst requiring a huge concentration of organisational effort and resources. Colloquially, some councils that are known for their ability to score highly in performance terms are known as 'cappuccino councils', being consistent with a culture that emphasises froth over substance, or 'looking good' over 'being good' (Barnes, 2004). Continued evolution would also require clearer articulation of a value base in the wider system which acknowledges the implicit motivation of staff, prioritises genuine partnership with users and carers, and focuses on the strengths and capacities of all stakeholders, rather than having a fixation on what is not working and a tendency towards blame.

Implementation of personalisation has significant implications for relationships between staff, users and carers. Interpretations of personalisation, and the role of outcomes, show variation across England, Scotland and Wales. In England in particular, there has been a wholesale policy emphasis on self-directed support as the mainstream approach to social care provision, as outlined in *Putting People First* (DH, 2008). However, despite promises of progress in person-centredness from self-directed support, recent research has shown that personalisation has been located within traditional policy arrangements, rather than challenging them. The research highlighted that an effective approach to achieving person-centred support:

- is likely to require systemic change;
- will be rights-based and needs-led, in line with an independent living philosophy;
- can make some progress through bottom-up approaches, without broader reform, but this is likely to be limited, insecure and constrained;
- needs a stable context; the constant churn of organisational and external change makes it difficult to sustain bottom-up developments;
- needs commitment at every level;
- requires the development of forums for collective involvement and opportunities for capacity-building for all key stakeholders: these are key for participatory change to be possible;
- takes a long time, longer than might be expected. (Joseph Rowntree Foundation, 2011)

The findings of the Joseph Rowntree research are consistent with the experience of implementing outcomes-based working. Outcomes can also be consistent with the rights-based approaches advocated by the research, depending on how outcomes are interpreted.

From managerialism to a relationships-based approach

This book has been structured to explore outcomes from the various perspectives in the system, because the perspectives need to be aligned for outcomes-based working to be effective. The premise is that there are two competing interpretations of outcomes at work in practice. One fits with the managerialist paradigm and the other with the democratic citizenship/relationship-based one. In keeping with the latter approach, what matters to people has to be the starting point, and systems and processes need to be aligned to fit with that (see Table 6.1).

In the early chapters of this book, discussion centred round some of the tensions inherent in the health and social care system. This included evidence of how barriers to effective communication and partnership are raised by 'below the waterline' policy and agency requirements to restrict access to services, which sit in contradiction with the consumerist rhetoric espoused in formal policy. Reviewing evidence on the importance of relationships in public services, Bell

Table 6.1: Managerialist and democratic relationship-based approaches compared.

	Managerialist approach	Democratic relationship-based approach
Value base	Market driven	Public sector driven
	Deficit focus	Strengths focus
	Primary focus on 'proving' outcomes	Primary focus on 'improving' outcomes
	Medical model predominant	Social model predominant
	Primarily values efficiency and effectiveness	Also values justice and fairness
Perception of service user/ carer	Individual as demanding consumer with an emphasis on 'choice'	Individual as active citizen with an emphasis on 'voice'
Role of assessment	Emphasis on procedural assessment as a means of determining access and gathering performance data	Emphasis on a cycle of assessment, planning and review to ensure relevance of support from the user perspective
Form of interaction	Interactions are procedurally driven	Interactions are relationship based
Demand management	Manage demand by bureaucratic means	Manage demand by enabling the individual to be as involved and independent as possible
Purpose	Endpoint is delivery of a package of care	Endpoint is involvement of the person in partnership with services in meeting outcomes
Management style	Effective management	Emotionally intelligent leadership at all levels
Roles of performance management	Centrally determined performance management of staff	Staff, user and carer perspectives included in determining meaningful measures
	Performance management driven by competition and comparison with others	Performance management driven primarily by concern to understand and improve locally
How staff are perceived	Staff require extrinsic control	Staff as intrinsically motivated

and Smerdon (2011) found that relationships and outcomes-based working could play a vital role in helping to negotiate through these complexities. Evidence from England, Wales and Scotland also demonstrates the potential of outcomes-based working to improve partnership and more enabling relationships between staff and service users and carers (Miller, 2010), based on a more mature notion of the relationship between public services and citizens. Indeed, research in this area shows that the public already have a more sophisticated conceptualisation of their relationship with public services than consumerist-oriented policy assumes (Newman and Clarke, 2009). Underneath these concerns, it is imperative that paternalism in health and social services should be overcome, as it remains the Achilles heel of the public sector in face of globalising tendencies.

Cautionary note: The Big Society

The most recent market-oriented prescription for public sector paternalism is the notion of Building the Big Society. This was the first major policy announcement from the newly elected Coalition government in May 2010. The policy sets out four principles (2010):

- give communities more powers;
- encourage people to take an active role in their communities;
- transfer power from central to local government;
- support co-ops, mutuals, charities and social enterprises.

The concept of the Big Society, though somewhat loosely defined, relates to previous models of community development or community capacity building. However, there is also a significant emphasis by the Coalition government on a transfer from public service provision to the independent sector. There are significant risks attached with this agenda. One risk concerns the formalising of voluntary activity within communities, resulting in individuals feeling pressurised and retreating (Coote, 2010). Fragmentation raises questions of accountability and risks of returning to 'inadequate, partial and muddled patchworks' service provision as existed prior to the welfare state (Klein, 1995, p. 1). Coote (2010, p. 3) summarises a range of concerns as follows:

> We move from pooling responsibility through the machinery of a democratic state to dividing it between individuals, groups, localities and organisations in the private and voluntary sectors. It is not clear how the rights of individuals

will be protected, essential services guaranteed, or those who are poor, powerless and marginalised defended against those who are better off.

Policy claims that the voluntary sector has an exclusive capacity to innovate ignores the wealth of innovation taking place within the public sector. Further to this, the capacity of the voluntary sector to innovate can be stifled in a highly competitive market-driven culture, as contracts are increasingly squeezed (Pollock *et al.*, 2008). Work by Mark Moore (1995) shows how 'public value' can be instituted as an organising principle in a public sector organisation, in the context of which individual employees are free to pursue and propose new ideas about how to improve the working of the organisation, in terms of efficiency of services. The third sector does contain knowledge and expertise which should be more fully taken into consideration in the wider policy-making arena. It has been noted, however, that relationships between the public and third sectors have been characterised by tension (Andrews *et al.*, 2009). Perhaps the tension could be reduced by a more clearly defined policy vision at the centre, with a clearer view of the role of and boundaries between sectors.

Conclusion

The considerable improvement potential of outcomes-based working is emerging across the UK, with the chance to move towards management of demand based on best practice and more effective use of resources. It has been argued, based on experience, that outcomes-focused assessment can support more people without necessarily using more resources (Slasberg, 2010). Notwithstanding the efficiencies of outcomes-based working, however, it remains the case that social care in particular requires sufficient funding to achieve person-centred goals, with a recent case made for adequate funding from general taxation as likely to offer the most effective route to achieve 'person-centred support' and to reduce the increasingly unhelpful barriers between health, social care and other services (Joseph Rowntree Foundation, 2011).

Outcomes-based working requires more honest communication, and a focus on maximising the potential of each individual rather than responding to consumerist demand and a tendency do to things to rather than with people. The associated emphasis on the importance of relationships is not a luxurious 'extra' confined to pockets within the system, but is fundamental to a health and social care system that works, is efficient and delivers good outcomes to individuals. An additional appeal of outcomes-based working is its potential to improve alignment and integration in the system through articulation of a common language, which can also help to reinforce that people's outcomes are basically the same, whether a member of staff, service user and/or carer.

The challenge, however, is the requirement for wider systems to realign around outcomes to enable and support outcomes-focused practice to be embedded at the front line. This means establishing a coherent value base articulated around what matters to people, and a focus on strengths and capacities rather than deficits, at all levels in the system. It also means moving from a culture of change for its own sake to change that is consistent with the shared value base, and a need for less hyperactive policy-making at the centre. In particular, it means a reversal of the managerialising tendencies which have come to predominate in health and social care systems, to promote rather than impede the growth of enabling relationships.

REFERENCES

Abendstern, M., Clarkson, P., Challis, D. J., Hughes, J. and Sutcliffe, C. L. (2008) 'Implementing the single assessment process for older people in England: Lessons from the literature', *Research, Policy and Planning*, Vol. 26, No. 1, pp. 15–32

Akeriordet, K. and Severinsson, E. (2008) 'Emotionally intelligent nurse leaders', *Journal of Nurse Management*, Vol. 16, No. 5, pp. 565–77

Aldred, H. and Gott, M. (2005) 'Advanced heart failure: Impact on older patients and informal carers', *Journal of Advanced Nursing*, Vol. 49, No. 2, pp. 116–24

Allsop, J. (1995) *Health Policy and the NHS*, London: Longman

Andrews, N., Driffield, D. and Poole, V. (2009) 'A collaborative and relationship-centred approach to improving assessment and care management with older people in Swansea', *Quality in Ageing*, Vol. 10, No. 3, pp. 12–23

Antonakis, J. (2009). ' "Emotional intelligence": What does it measure and does it matter for leadership?', in Graen, G. B. (ed.) (2009) *LMX Leadership — Game-Changing Designs: Research-Based Tools*, Vol. 7, pp. 163–92, Greenwich, CT: Information Age Publishing

Audit Commission (2002) *Recruitment and Retention — A Public Service Workforce for the 20th Century*, London: Audit Commission

Audit Commission (2004) *The Effectiveness and Cost-Effectiveness of Support and Services to Informal Carers of Older People*, London: Audit Commission

Austin, E. J. (2008) 'A reaction time study of responses to trait and ability emotional intelligence test items', *Personality and Individual Differences*, Vol. 36, pp. 1855–64

Ball, S., Mudd, J., Oxley, M., Pinnock, M., Qureshi, H. and Nicholas, E. (2004) 'Make outcomes your big idea: Using outcomes to refocus social care practice and information', *Journal of Integrated Care*, Vol. 12, pp. 13–19

Barnes, C. (2002) 'Introduction: Disability, policy and politics', *Policy and Politics*, Vol. 30, No. 3, pp. 311–18

Barnes, J. (2004) 'Waving, or drowning? Tackling performance in local authority social services', *Research, Policy and Planning*, Vol. 22, No. 3, pp. 61–9

Barnes, M. and Prior, D. (1995) 'Spoilt for choice? How consumerism can disempower public service users', *Public Money and Management*, July–September, pp. 53–9

Bauld, L., Chesterman, J., Davies, B., Judge, K. and Mangalore, R. (2000) *Caring for Older People: An Assessment of Community Care in the 1990s*, Aldershot: Aldgate

Baxter, K., Rabiee, P. and Glendinning, C. (2011) *Choice and Change: Disabled Adults' and Older People's Experiences of Making Choice about Services and*

Support, York: SPRU

Bell, K. and Smerdon, M. (2011) *Deep Value: A Literature Review of the Role of Effective Relationships in Public Services*. Available from URL: www.community-links.org/uploads/editor/DeepValueSeminar.pdf (accessed 6 July 2011)

Benner P. (1984) *From Novice to Expert: Excellence and Power in Clinical Nursing Practice*, Menlo Park, Calif.: Addison-Wesley

Beresford, P. (2008) 'Whose personalisation?', *Soundings*, Vol. 40, pp. 8–17

Bevan, G. and Hood, C. (2006) 'Have targets improved performance in the English NHS?', *British Medical Journal*, Vol. 332, pp. 419–122

Blair, T. (2003) 'We must not waste this precious period of power', Tony Blair speaking at South Camden Community College, London, 23 January 2003

Boyle, D. and Harris, M. (2009) *The Challenge of Co-production*, London: Nesta

Broadhurst, K., Wastell, D., White, S., Hall, C., Peckover, S., Thompson, K., Pithouse, A. and Davey, D. (2010) 'Performing "initial assessment": Identifying the latent conditions for error at the front-door of local authority children's services', *British Journal of Social Work*, Vol. 40, pp. 352–70

Brodie, I., Nottingham, C. and Plunkett, S. (2008) 'A tale of two reports: Social work in Scotland from "Social work and the community" (1966) to "Changing lives" (2006)', *British Journal of Social Work*, Vol. 38, pp. 697–715

Bruce, A. and Forbes, T. (2005) 'Delivering community care in Scotland: Are local partnership agreements the answer', *Scottish Affairs*, Vol. 52, pp. 89–109

Burnham, D. (2006) *Only Get Better? A Guide to Social Services Performance Measurement Processes for Front Line Staff*, Lyme Regis: Russell House Publishing

Burns, H. (2009) *Health in Scotland 2009: Time for Change*, annual report of the chief medical officer, Edinburgh: Scottish Government

Campbell, J. and Oliver, M. (1996) *Disability Politics: Understanding our Past, Changing our Future*, London: Routledge

Carers UK (2003) *Missed Opportunities: The Impact of New Rights for Carers*, London: Carers UK

Carers UK (2008) *Carers in Crisis: A Survey of Carers Finances in 2008*, London: Carers UK

Carr, S. (2010) *Enabling Risk, Ensuring Safety: Self-directed Support and Personal Budgets*, London: Social Care Institute for Excellence

Cavaye, J. (2006) *Hidden Carers*, Edinburgh: Dunedin

CCPS (2002) *A Joint Future for Community Care: A Voluntary Sector Perspective*, Edinburgh: Community Care Providers Scotland

Challis, D. (1993) 'Care management: Observations from a programme of research', *PSSRU Bulletin 9*, Canterbury: University of Kent, pp. 33–4

Clarke, J. and Newman, J. (1997) *The Managerial State*, London: Sage

Clarkson, M. (2009) 'Leadership and management in nursing: Concepts analysis'. Masters dissertation available from http://researcharchive.wintec.ac.nz/532/1/Research_Project_2009_HLNU902_FINAL.pdf (accessed 22 January 2011)

Clarkson, P. (2010) 'Performance measurement in adult social care: Looking backwards and forwards', *British Journal of Social Work*, Vol. 40, pp. 170–87

Clements, L. (2011) 'Social care law developments: A sideways look at personalisation and tightening eligibility criteria' (presented for publication).

Available from URL: www.lukeclements.co.uk/downloads/ElderLawArticle2011.pdf (accessed 10 April 2011)

Cohen, G., Forbes, J., Garraway, M. (1996) 'Can different patient satisfaction survey methods yield consistent results? Comparison of three surveys,' *British Medical Journal*, Vol. 313, pp. 814–4

Cook, A. (2008) *Dementia and Well-being: Possibilities and Challenges,* Edinburgh: Dunedin

Cook, A. and Miller, E. (2010) *Talking Points: Personal Outcomes Approach Update Report June 2010: Focus on Making Use of Information on Outcomes,* Edinburgh: Joint Improvement Team. Available from www.jitscotland.org.uk/action-areas/talking-points-user-and-carer-involvement/using-outcomes-data (accessed 6 July 2011)

Cook, A., Miller, E. and Whoriskey, M. (2007) *Do Health and Social Care Partnerships Deliver Good Outcomes to Service Users and Carers? Development of the User Defined Service Evaluation Toolkit* (UDSET), Edinburgh: Joint Improvement Team

Cooksey, D. (2006) *A Review of UK Health Research Funding,* Norwich: HMSO

Coote, A. (2010) *Cutting It: The 'Big Society' and the New Austerity,* London: New Economics Foundation

Crerar, L. (2007) *Report of the Independent Review of Regulation, Audit, Inspection and Complaints Handling of Public Services in Scotland,* Edinburgh: The Scottish Government

CSCI (2004) *Leaving Hospital: The Price of Delays,* London: Commission for Social Care Inspection

CSCI (2006) *Time to Care: An Overview of home care services for older people in England,* London: Commission for Social Care Inspection

CSCI (2008) *Performance Summary Report of 2007–08 Annual Performance Assessment of Social Care Services for Adults Services for Thurrock Burrough Council,* London: Commission for Social Care Inspection

Cutler, T. and Waine, B. (1994) *Managing the Welfare State,* London: Berg

de Bruijn, H. (2002) 'Performance measurement in the public sector: Strategies to cope with the risks of performance measurement', *The International Journal of Public Sector Management,* Vol. 15, No. 7, pp. 578–94

DH (1989) *Caring for People,* London: Department of Health

DH (1990) *National Health and Community Care Act,* London: Department of Health

DH (1995) *Carers (Recognition and Services) Act,* London: Department of Health

DH (1998) *Modernising Adult Social Care Services,* London: The Stationery Office

DH (2000) *Carers and Disabled Children Act: Carers and People with Parental Responsibilities for Disabled Children, Practice Guidance,* London: Department of Health

DH (2005) *Independence, Well-being and Choice: Our Vision for the Future of Adult Social Care in England,* London: The Stationery Office

DH (2006) *Our Health, Our Care, Our Say: A New Direction for Community Services,* London: Department of Health

DH (2008) *Putting People First,* London: Department of Health

DH (2009) *Caring with Confidence: Preliminary Research Amongst Carers to Inform and Shape a New Expert Carers-Type Programme,* Leeds: Caring with Confidence

DH (2010) *Transparency in Outcomes — A Framework for the NHS,* London: Department of Health

DH (2011) *Transparency in Outcomes — A Framework for Quality in Adult Social Care,* London: Department of Health

DHSS (1981) *Growing Older,* London: HMSO

DH/SSI (1991) *Care Management and Assessment: Managers Guide,* London: HMSO

Dickinson, H. (2008) *Evaluating Outcomes in Health and Social Care,* Bristol: Policy Press

Drewett, A. (1999) 'Social rights and disability: The language of "rights" in community care policies, *Disability and Society,* Vol. 14, No. 1, pp. 115–28

Dunning, J. (2010) 'Scotland makes self-directed support central to social care', *Community Care,* 15 March 2010. Available from URL: www.communitycare.co.uk/Articles/2010/03/15/114050/Personalisation-in-Scotland.htm (accessed 14 March 2011)

Eccles, A. (2008) 'Single shared assessment: The limits to "Quick fix" implementation', *Journal of Integrated Care,* Vol. 16, No. 1, pp. 23–30

Evans, T. and Harris, J. (2004) 'Street-level bureaucracy, social work and the (exaggerated) death of discretion', *British Journal of Social Work,* Vol. 34, No. 6, pp. 871–95

Ferlie, E. and Steane, P. (2002) 'Changing developments in NPM', *International Journal of Public Administration,* Vol. 25, No. 12, pp. 1459–69

Fine, M. and Glendinning, C. (2005) 'Dependence, independence or interdependence? Revisiting the concepts of "care" and "dependency" ', *Ageing and Society,* Vol. 25, No. 4, pp. 601–21

Forbes, T. and Evans, D. (2008) 'Health and social care partnerships in Scotland', *Scottish Affairs,* Vol. 65, pp. 87–106

Fox, D., Holder, J. and Netten, A. (2009) '*Carers' experience survey 2009–10: Survey development project, PSSRU discussion paper 2643*', University of Kent, Canterbury: Personal Social Services Unit

Fyffe, T. (2009) '*Response to consultation on healthcare quality strategy for Scotland — draft strategy document,*' Edinburgh: Royal College of Nursing Scotland

Gillies, B (2000) 'Acting up: Ambiguity and the legal recognition of carers', *Ageing and Society,* Vol. 20, Pt 4, pp. 429–44

Glasby, J. (2003) *Hospital Discharge: Integrating Health and Social Care,* Abingdon: Radcliffe Medical Press

Glendinning, C., Clarke, S., Hare, P., Kotchetkova, I., Maddison, J. and Newbronner, L. (2006) *Outcomes-Focused Services for Older People,* Bristol: The Policy Press

Glendinning, C., Clarke, S., Hare, P., Kotchetkova, I., Maddison, J. and Newbronner, L. (2008) 'Progress and problems in developing outcomes-focused social care services for older people in England', *Health and Social Care in the Community,* Vol. 16, No. 1, pp. 54–63

Godfrey, M. and Denby, T. (2004) *Depression and Older People: Towards Securing Well-being in Later Life.* Bristol: Policy Press

Goffman, E. (1974) *Frame Analysis: An Essay on the Organisation of Experience,* New York: Harper and Row

Goleman, D., Boyatzis, R. and McKee, A. (2002) *Primal Leadership,* Boston, Harvard Business School Press

Gooday, K. and Stewart, A. (2009) 'Community care and the Single Outcome Agreement in Scotland: A driver or barrier to better outcomes?', *Journal of Integrated Care,* Vol. 17, No. 5, pp. 31–7

Guberman, N., Nicholas, E., Nolan, M. Rembicki, D., Lundh, U. and Keefe, J. (2003) 'Impacts on practitioners of using research-based carer assessment tools: Experiences from the UK, Canada and Sweden, with insights from Australia', *Health and Social Care in the Community,* Vol. 11, No. 4, pp. 345–55

Handley, P. (2000) 'Trouble in paradise — a disabled person's right to the satisfaction of a self-define need: Some conceptual and practical problems', *Disability and Society,* Vol. 15, No. 2, pp. 313–25

Hanson, E., Nolan, J., Magnusson, L., Sennemark, E., Johansson, L. and Nolan, M. (2006) *COAT: The Carers Outcome Agreement Tool,* Sheffield: Getting Research Into Practice

Hardy, B., Hudson, B. and Waddington, E. (2000) *What Makes a Good Partnership? A Partnership Assessment Tool,* Leeds: Nuffield Institute

Harris, J. (2002) 'Caring for citizenship', *British Journal of Social Work,* Vol. 32, No. 3, pp. 267–81

Hart, M. (1999) 'The quantification of patient satisfaction', in Davies, H., Malek, M. and Neilson, A. (eds) *Managing Quality and Controlling Costs: Strategic Issues in Health Care Management,* Surrey: Ashgate, Chapter 6, pp. 68–88

Henderson, J. (2001) ' "He's not my carer — he's my husband": Personal and policy constructions of care in mental health', *Journal of Social Work Practice,* Vol. 15, No. 2, pp. 149–59

Henwood, M. (2001) *Future Imperfect: Report of the Kings Fund Care and Support Inquiry,* London: Kings Fund

Hirst, M. (2005) 'Carer distress: A prospective, population-based study', *Social Science and Medicine,* Vol. 61, No. 3, pp. 697–708

Hitchins, S. (2010) *Talking Points: A Personal Outcomes Approach: An Evaluation of the Midlothian Pilots.* Available from URL: www.jitscotland.org.uk/action-areas/talking-points-user-and-carer-involvement/evidence-learning-and-the-community-of-practice (accessed 10 July 2011)

HM Treasury (2003) *Every Child Matters,* London: The Stationery Office

Hoggett, P. (1996) 'New modes of control in public service', *Public Administration,* Vol. 74, pp. 9–32

Home Office (2003) *Building Civil Renewal,* London: Home Office

Hudson, B. (2011) 'Ten years of jointly commissioning health and social care in England', *International Journal of Integrated Care,* Special 10th anniversary edn

Hugman, R. (1994) 'Social work and case management in the UK: Models of professionalism and elderly people', *Ageing and Society,* Vol. 14, No. 2, pp. 237–53

Iles, V. and Sutherland, L. (2001) '*Managing Change in the NHS: Organisational*

Change, A Review for Health Care Managers, Professionals and Researchers', London: NHS Service Delivery and Organisation

Improvement Service (2011) *The Outcomes Challenge*, Broxburn: The Improvement Service

Independent Commission on Social Services in Wales (2010) *From Vision to Action: The Report of the Independent Commission on Social Services in Wales*, Cardiff: Welsh Assembly Government

Institute of Public Care (2009) *Transforming the Market For Social Care: Changing the Currency of Commissioning from outputs to outcomes*. Available from URL: www.dhcarenetworks.org.uk/_library/Resources/BetterCommissioning/whatsNew/market_facilitation_paper4.pdf (accessed 6 July 2011)

Jarvis, A. (2010) 'Working with carers in the next decade: The challenges', *British Journal of Community Nursing*, Vol. 15, No. 3, pp. 125–8

Johnston, J. and Miller, E. (2010) *Staff Support and Supervision for Outcomes-Based Working*, Edinburgh: Joint Improvement Team

Jordan, B. (2007) *Social Work and Well-being*, Dorset: Russell House Publishing

Joseph Rowntree Foundation (2011) *Transforming Social Care: Sustaining Person-Centred Support*, York: Joseph Rowntree Foundation

Kendall, J. (1999) 'The voluntary sector and social care for older people', in Hudson, B. (ed.) (2000) *The Changing Role of Social Care*, Aberdeen: Robert Gordon University

Keynes, John Maynard (1936) *The General Theory of Employment, Interest and Money*, London: Macmillan (reprinted 2007)

Klein, R. (1995) *The New Politics of the NHS*, Essex: Longman

Laming, H. (2009) *The Protection of Children in England: A Progress Report*, London, House of Commons

Leadbetter, C. (2004) *Personalisation through Participation: A New Script for Public Services*, London: Demos

Le Grand, J. (1997) 'Knights, knaves or pawns: Human behaviour and social policy', *Journal of Social Policy*, Vol. 26, No. 2, pp. 149–69

Lewin, K. (1951) *Field Theory in Social Science*, New York: Harper and Row

Lewis, J. and Glennerster, H. (1996) *Implementing the New Community Care*, Buckingham: Open University Press

Leys, C. (2003) *Market Driven Politics*, London: Verso

Lipsky, M. (1980) *Street Level Bureaucracy: Dilemmas of the Individual in Public Services*, New York: Russell Sage Foundation

Lloyd, M. (2001) 'The politics of disability and feminism: Discord or synthesis?' *Sociology*, Vol. 35, No. 3, pp. 715–28

Lyons, M. (2007) 'Place-shaping: A shared ambition for the future of local government', *Final Report*, London: The Stationery Office

McAdam, R., Hazlett, S.-A. and Casey, C. (2005) 'Performance management in the UK public sector: Addressing multiple stakeholder complexity', *The International Journal of Public Sector Management*, Vol. 18, No. 3, pp. 256–72

McAteer, M. and Bennett, M. (2005) 'Devolution and local government: Evidence from Scotland', *Local Government Studies*, Vol. 31, No. 3, pp. 285–306

MacIntyre, G. (2008) *Learning Disability and Social Inclusion*, Edinburgh: Dunedin

McNally, D., Cornes, M. and Clough, R. (2003) 'Implementing the single assessment process: Driving change or expecting the impossible?', *Journal of Integrated Care*, Vol. 11, No. 2, pp. 9–18

McNamara, G. (2006) 'Implementation of single shared assessment in Meadowbank, Falkirk: A joint future', *Journal of Integrated Care*, Vol. 14, No. 4, pp. 38–44

McPhail, M. (2008) *Service User and Carer Involvement: Beyond Good Intentions*, Edinburgh: Dunedin

Martin, G. P., Phelps, K. and Katbamna, S. (2004) 'Human motivation and professional practice: Of knights, knaves and social workers', *Social Policy and Administration*, Vol. 38, No. 5, pp. 470–87

Means, R., Richards, S. and Smith, R. (2008) *Community Care*, Hampshire: Palgrave Macmillan

Miller, E. (2007) *Identifying the Outcomes Important to Unpaid Carers*, Edinburgh: Joint Improvement Team

Miller, E. (2010) 'Can the shift from needs-led to outcomes-focused assessment in health and social care deliver on policy priorities?', *Research, Policy and Planning*, Vol. 28, No. 2, pp. 115–27

Miller, E. (2011) *Good Conversations: Assessment and Planning as the Building Blocks of an Outcomes Approach*, Edinburgh: Joint Improvement Team

Miller, E. and Cameron, K. (2011) 'Challenges and benefits in implementing shared assessment across the UK: A literature review', *Journal of Interprofessional Care*, Vol. 25, No. 1, pp. 39–45

Miller, E., Cook, A., Samet, W. (2009) *Philosophy and Principles Underpinning a Personal Outcomes Approach*, Edinburgh: Joint Improvement Team

Miller, E. and Johnstone, J. (2008) *Outcomes in Practice: A Report on Focus Groups with Social Work Practitioners, Seniors and Managers in North Lanarkshire*, Edinburgh: Joint Improvement Team and North Lanarkshire Council

Miller, E., Whoriskey, M. and Cook, A. (2008) 'Outcomes for users and carers in the context of health and social care partnership working: From research to practice', *Journal of Integrated Care*, Vol. 16, No. 2, pp. 19–26

Mintzberg, H. (1983) *Structure in Fives: Designing Organisational Effectiveness*, London: Prentice-Hall

Moore, M. (1995) *Creating Public Value: Strategic Management in Government*, Cambridge, Mass.: Harvard University Press

Moroney, R. (1976) *The Family and the State*, London: Longman

Morris, J. (1993) *Community Care or Independent Living*, York: Joseph Rowntree Foundation/London: Community Care

Morris, J. (2004) 'Independent living and community care: A disempowering framework', *Disability and Society*, Vol. 19, No. 5, pp. 427–42

Morrison, T. (2007) 'Emotional intelligence, emotion and social work: _Context, characteristics, complications and contribution', *British Journal of Social Work*, Vol. 37, pp. 245–63

Moynihan, R. and Henry, D. (2006) 'The fight against disease mongering: Generating knowledge for action'. Available from URL: www.ploscollections.org/article/info:doi%2F10.1371%2Fjournal.pmed.0030191 (accessed 15 April 2011)

Munro, E. (2011) 'A child centred system'. Available form URL: www.educa-tion.gov.uk/munroreview/recommendations.shtml (accessed 2 June 2011)

Murphy, J., Gray, C. M., Cox, S., van Achterberg, T. and Wyke, S. (2010) 'The effectiveness of the talking mats framework with people with dementia', *Dementia : International Journal of Social research and Practice*, Vol. 9, No. 4, pp. 454–72

Needham, C. (2010) *Commissioning for Personalization: From the Fringes to the Mainstream*, CIPFA: London

Newman, J. (2005) 'Modernising adult social care: Researching the impact of reform on service users', *Journal of Integrated Care*, Vol. 13, No. 6, pp. 13–16

Newman, J. and Clarke, J. (2009) *Publics, Politics and Power: Remaking the Public in Public Services*, London: Sage

NHS: SDO (2010) *The Impact of Incentives on the Behaviour and Performance of Primary Care Professionals*, London: HMSO

Nicholas, E. (2003) 'An outcomes focus in carer assessment and review: Value and challenges', *British Journal of Social Work*, Vol. 33, No. 1, pp. 31–47

Nicholas, E., Qureshi, H. and Bamford, C. (2003) *Outcomes into Practice: Focusing Practice and information on the Outcomes People Value*, York: SPRU

Niskanen, W. A. (1971) *Bureaucracy and Representative Government*, New York: Aldine-Atherton

Nolan, M., Brown, J., Davies, S., Nolan, J. and Keady, J. (2006) *The Senses Framework: Improving Care for Older People Through a Relationship Centred Approach*, Getting Research into Practice (GRiP) Report No. 2. Sheffield: University of Sheffield

Patmore, C. and McNulty, A. (2005) *Flexible, Person-Centred Home Care for Older People*, York: SPRU

Payer, L. (1992) *Disease-Mongers: How Doctors, Drug Companies, and Insurers Are Making You Feel Sick*, New York: Wiley

Petch, A. (2008) *Health and Social Care: Establishing a Joint Future?* Edinburgh: Dunedin

Petch, A. (2011) An Evidence Base for the Delivery of Adult Services: Report Commissioned by ADSW, Glasgow: IRISS

Petch, A., Cook, A. and Miller, E. (2005) 'Focusing on outcomes: Their role in partnership policy and practice', *Journal of Integrated Care*, Vol. 13, No. 6, pp. 3–12

Petch, A., Cook, A., Miller, E., Alexander, H. E., Cooper, A., Hubbard, G. and Morrison, J. (2007) *Users and Carers Define Effective Partnerships in Health and Social Care*. Available from URL: www.jitscotland.org.uk/action-areas/themes/involvement.html (accessed 2 February 2011)

Pollitt, C. (1994) 'The citizens charter: A preliminary analysis', *Public Money and Management*, Vol. 12, pp. 9–14

Pollock, A., Price, D., Miller, E., Viebrock, E., Shaoul, J. and Mohan, J. (2008) *A Literature Review on the Structure and Performance of Not-for-Profit Health Care Organisations* (SDO.106.20005) London: NHS Service Delivery and Organisation

Postle, K. (2001) 'Things fall apart: The centre cannot hold: Deconstructing and reconstructing social work with older people for the twenty-first century',

Issues in Social Work Education, Vol. 19, No. 2, pp. 23–43

Postle, K. (2002) 'Working "Between the idea and the reality": Ambiguities and tensions in care managers' work', *British Journal of Social Work*, Vol. 32, No. 3, pp. 335–51

Postle, K. and Beresford, P. (2007) 'Capacity building and the re-conception of political participation: A role for social care workers?', *British Journal of Social Work*, Vol. 3, No. 1, pp. 143–58

Qureshi, H. (ed.) (2001) *Outcomes in Social Care Practice*, York: SPRU

Qureshi, H. and Nicholas, E. (2001) 'A new conception of social care outcomes and its practical use in assessment with older people', *Research, Policy and Planning*, Vol. 19, No. 2 pp. 11–26

Reid Howie (2010) *Short Break (Respite Care) Planning and Provision in Scotland*, Edinburgh: Reid Howie Associates

Rogers, E.M. (1995; 4th edn) *The Diffusion of Innovations*, New York: The Free Press

Rummery, K. (2002) *Disability, Citizenship and Community Care: A Case for Welfare Rights?* Aldershot: Ashgate

Rummery, K. and Glendinning, C. (1999) 'Negotiating needs, access and gatekeeping, developments in health and community care policies in the UK and the rights of disabled and older citizens', *Critical Social Policy*, Vol. 19, No. 3, pp. 335–51

Ryburn, B., Wells, Y. and Foreman, P. (2009) 'Enabling independence: Restorative approaches to home care provision for frail older adults', *Health and Social Care in the Community*, Vol. 17, No. 3, pp. 225–34

Samuel, M. (2011) 'Adult social care and health to be fused in Scotland', *Community Care*, 2 February 2011. Available from URL: www.communitycare. co.uk/Articles/2011/02/02/116210/adult-social-care-and-health-to-be-fused-in-scotland.htm (accessed 2 April 2011)

Sawyer, L. (2005) 'An outcomes-based approach to domiciliary care', *Journal of Integrated Care*, Vol. 13, No. 3, pp. 20–5

Scottish Executive (2002) *Community Care and Health (Scotland) Act*, Edinburgh: Scottish Executive

Scottish Executive (2003) *Report of the JPIAF SSA Performance Measures Subgroup: Performance Measures for Carers' Assessments — Consultation Paper*, Edinburgh: Scottish Executive

Scottish Executive (2005) *Better Outcomes for Older People — A Framework for Joint Services for Older People*, Edinburgh: Scottish Executive, Joint Services Group

Scottish Executive (2006) *Changing Lives: Report of the C21st Social Work Review*, Edinburgh: The Stationery Office

Scottish Executive (2007a) *CEL/National Outcomes for Community Care, 4 July 2007*, Edinburgh: The Scottish Executive

Scottish Executive (2007b) *National Guidance on Self-Directed Support*, Scottish Government Circular CCD7/2007, Edinburgh: The Stationery Office

Scottish Government (2007a) *Better Health, Better Care*, Edinburgh: The Stationery Office

Scottish Government (2007b) *Concordat between the Scottish Government and*

Local Government, Edinburgh: Scottish Government and COSLA

Scottish Government (2008) *National Minimum Standards for Assessment, Care Planning and Review,* Edinburgh: The Scottish Government

Scottish Government (2010a) *The Healthcare Quality Strategy for NHS Scotland,* Edinburgh: The Scottish Government

Scottish Government (2010b) *Caring Together: The Carers Strategy 2010–15,* Edinburgh: The Scottish Government

Scottish Government (2011) *Reshaping Care for Older People: A Programme for Change, 2011–2021,* Edinburgh: The Scottish Government

Scottish Office (1998) *Modernising Community Care: An Action Plan,* Edinburgh: The Stationery Office

Seddon, D. and Robinson, C. (2001) 'Carers of older people with dementia: Assessment and the Carers Act', *Journal of Health and Social Care in the Community,* Vol. 9, No. 3, pp. 151–8

Seddon, D., Robinson, C. and Perry, J. (2010) 'Unified assessment: Policy, implementation and practice', *British Journal of Social Work,* Vol. 40, pp. 207–25

Seddon, D., Robinson, C., Reeves, C., Tommis, Y., Woods, B. and Russell, I. (2006) 'In their own right: Translating the policy of carer assessment into practice', *British Journal of Social Work,* Vol. 37, No. 8, pp. 1335–52

Seddon, J. (2008) *Systems Thinking in the Public Sector: The Failure of the Reform Regime … And a Manifesto for a Better Way,* Axminster: Triarchy Press

Slasberg, C. (2010) 'Reablement, efficiency and outcomes working', *Journal of Care Services Management,* Vol. 4, No. 2, pp. 141–9

Smale, G. (1996) *Mapping Change and Innovation,* National Institute for Social Work Practice, London: HMSO

Smale, G. (1998) *Managing Change through Innovation,* London: National Institute for Social Work, London: HMSO

Smale, G., Tuson, G., Biehal, N. and Marsh, P. (1993) *Empowerment, Assessment, Care Management and the Skilled Worker,* National Institute for Social Work Practice and Development Exchange, London: HMSO

Stanton, E. and Noble, D. (2010) 'Emotional intelligence', *British Medical Journal,* 17 November 2010. Available from URL: http://bmjcareers.mobi/careers/advice/view-article.html?id=20001646 (accessed 23 January 2011)

Stewart, A. (2008) *An Evaluation of UDSET in the Pilot Sites,* Edinburgh: Joint Improvement Team

Stock, C. and Lambert, S. (2011) 'Who care wins? Carers experiences of assessment since the introduction of the Carers (Equal Opportunities) Act 2004', *Research, Policy and Planning,* Vol. 28, No. 3, pp. 173–84

Sullivan, M. (2009) 'Social workers in community care practice: Ideologies and interactions with older people', *British Journal of Social Work,* Vol. 39, pp. 1306–25

Tizard, J. (2010) 'Afterword', in Needham, C. *Commissioning for Personalization: From the Fringes to the Mainstream,* London: CIPFA

Townsend, P. (1968) 'Ageing and social policy', in Phillipson, C. and Walker, A. (eds) *Ageing and Social Policy: A Critical Assessment.* Aldershot: Gower, pp. 15–44

Townsend, P. (1981) 'The structured dependency of the elderly: The creation of social policy in the 20th century', *Ageing and Society,* Vol. 1, No. 1, pp. 5–28

Tudor Hart, J. (2006) *The Political Economy of Health Care,* Bristol: The Policy Press

Ungerson, C. (1987) *Policy is Personal,* London: Tavistock

Upton, A. (2010) 'Exploring the effectiveness of collaborative inquiry in implementing an outcomes approach'. Dissertation for MSc at the University of Dundee

Van Thiel, S. and Leeuw, F. (2002) 'The performance paradox in the public sector', *Public Performance and Management Review,* Vol. 25, No. 3, pp. 267–81

Waine, B. and Henderson, J. (2003) 'Managers, managing and manageralism', in Henderson, J. and Atkinson, A. (eds) (2003) *Managing Care in Context,* London: Routledge

Ware, T., Matosevic, T., Hardy, B., Knapp, M., Kendall, J. and Forder, J. (2003) 'Commissioning care services for older people in England: The view from care managers, users and carers', *Ageing and Society,* Vol. 23, No. 4, pp. 411–28

Webb, S. A. (2006) *Social Work in a Risk Society: Social and Political Perspectives,* Basingstoke: Palgrave Macmillan

Welsh Assembly (2011) *Sustainable Social Services for Wales — A Framework for Action,* Cardiff: Welsh Assembly Government. Available from URL: http://wales.gov.uk/topics/health/publications/socialcare/guidance1/services/?lang=en (accessed 6 July 2011)

White, S., Wastell, D., Broadhurst, K. and Hall, C. (2010) 'When policy o'erleaps itself: The "tragic tale" of the integrated children's system', *Critical Social Policy,* Vol. 30, pp. 405–29

Williams, V. and Robinson, C. (2001) 'More than one wavelength: Identifying, understanding and resolving conflicts of interest between people with intellectual disabilities and their family carers', *Journal of Applied Research in Intellectual Disabilities,* Vol. 14, No. 1, pp. 30–46

Wistow, G., Knapp, M., Hardy, B., Forder, J., Kendall, J. and Manning, R. (1996) *Social Care Markets: Progress and Prospects,* Buckingham: Open University Press

Wyatt, M. (2002) 'Partnerships in health and social care: The implications of government guidance in the 1990s in England, with particular reference to voluntary organisations', *Policy and Politics,* Vol. 30, No. 2, pp. 167–82

Yoo, J. (2002) 'The relationship between organisational variables and client outcomes: A case study in child welfare', *Administration in Child Welfare,* Vol. 26, No. 2, pp. 39–61

Young, D. and Quibell, R. (2000) 'Why rights are never enough: Rights, intellectual disability and understanding', *Disability and Society,* Vol. 15, No. 5, pp. 747–64

INDEX

Note: page numbers in *italics* denote figures or tables